F6F HELLCAT
VS
A6M ZERO-SEN

Pacific Theater 1943–44

EDWARD M. YOUNG

First published in Great Britain in 2014 by Osprey Publishing
PO Box 883, Oxford, OX1 9PL, UK
PO Box 3985, New York, NY 10185–3985, USA
E-mail: info@ospreypublishing.com

A CIP catalogue record for this book is available from the British Library

ISBN: 978 1 78200 813 2

Edited by Tony Holmes
Cover artworks and battlescene by Gareth Hector (www.garethhector.co.uk/
aviation-art/)
Three-views, cockpits, armament scrap views and Engaging the Enemy
artwork by Jim Laurier
Index by Alan Thatcher
Maps by Bountford.com
Originated by PDQ Digital Media Solutions, UK
Printed in China through Asia Pacific Offset Limited

14 15 16 17 18   10 9 8 7 6 5 4 3 2 1

Osprey Publishing is supporting the Woodland Trust, the UK's leading
woodland conservation charity, by funding the dedication of trees.

www.ospreypublishing.com

Acknowledgments
I would like to express my gratitude to my good friend Osamu Tagaya for
sharing his insights into the duel between the F6F Hellcat and the A6M
Zero-sen. His observations gave me a better understanding of the
technological and industrial challenges Japan faced in its confrontation with
the United States. Sarah Serizawa translated portions from several Japanese
sources and memoirs of Zero-sen pilots describing their combats with the
Hellcat. The images for this volume came from the National Archives and
Records Administration (NARA), the National Naval Aviation Museum, the
Australian War Memorial and the Museum of Flight. I would like to thank
Holly Reed and her staff at NARA, Hill Goodspeed and his volunteers at the
National Naval Aviation Museum and Amy Heidrick at the Museum of Flight.
I would also like to acknowledge a debt to Frank Olynyk, whose vast research
on US Navy aerial victory claims during World War II was of inestimable
value to this volume.

F6F Hellcat cover art
Lt(jg) Eugene Hanks of VF-16 was the first Hellcat pilot to claim five Zero-
sens during a single mission. On November 23, 1943, Hanks was flying his
first mission as a division leader with VF-16, covering the landings on Tarawa
and Makin Islands. Responding to a call to intercept enemy aircraft, the
squadron climbed to 23,000ft and found a larger formation of Zero-sens
below them in a V-formation. Hanks dived down on a shotai of three fighters
that he identified as "Hamps", selecting the right wingman as his target.
Coming in from above at a "seven o'clock position", he opened fire, hitting the
"Hamp's" engine and then the wing root, the wing collapsing and folding up
under the impact of the Browning M-2 0.50in. rounds. In the ensuing fight
Hanks claimed two more "Hamps" and two Zero-sens in what was his first
aerial combat. Hellcat pilots would find that the Zero-sen flamed easily when
they could hit its vulnerable and unprotected fuel tanks in the wings. (Cover
artwork by Gareth Hector)

A6M Zero-sen cover art
Ens Yoshinao Kodaira was an experienced IJNAF fighter pilot who had
claimed his first victories flying over China. Assigned to the 601st Kokutai on
board the aircraft carrier *Shokaku* during the Battle of the Philippine Sea,
Kodaira was part of the escort of 48 Zero-sens supporting the second wave of
44 D4Y1 Suisei Carrier Bombers ("Judy") and 29 B6N2 Tenzan Carrier
Attack Bombers ("Jill") sent to attack Task Force 58 on June 19, 1944.
Although intercepting F6Fs tore the Japanese formation apart, Kodaira
managed to claim two Hellcats shot down before his own Zero-sen was hit
and he was forced to break away. He ditched in the sea and was rescued by an
IJN destroyer. Knocking down a Hellcat was no easy task, as the Zero-sen's
7.7mm machine guns had a limited effect on the rugged American fighter,
while the slower-firing 20mm cannon meant the IJNAF pilot could get off
fewer rounds in a quick burst. Accuracy was critical, and an experienced pilot
like Kodaira had a better chance of scoring a victory than most of his less well-
trained contemporaries flying at this late stage of the Pacific War. (Cover
artwork by Gareth Hector)

CONTENTS

INTRODUCTION

In the After Action Report he wrote following the Battle of Midway on June 4, 1942, Lt Cdr John Thach, CO of VF-3, was sharply critical of the performance of the Grumman F4F-4 Wildcat against the Mitsubishi A6M2 Zero-sen. The Wildcat, he wrote, was "pitifully inferior in climb, maneuverability and speed". Fortunately for the US Navy, the carrier fighter it needed to defeat the more nimble Zero-sen made its first flight just 22 days later at the Grumman factory in Bethpage, Long Island.

The F6F Hellcat, as it became known, was considered to be the finest carrier fighter of World War II. Superior in speed, rate of climb and maneuverability to the F4F Wildcat, ruggedly built and with a powerful engine and heavy armament, the Hellcat wrested air superiority from the vaunted Zero-sen within a few months of entering combat towards the end of 1943, establishing an ascendancy over its Japanese rival that it retained until the end of the war in the Pacific.

The duels between the Hellcat and the Zero-sen during 1943–44 represented a remarkable reversal of fortune. The Mitsubishi fighter had dominated the skies over Asia and the Pacific during the first year of combat that followed the attack on Pearl Harbor, outperforming most Allied fighters and meeting its match only when Allied pilots adopted tactics that negated the Zero-sen's superior maneuverability. The arrival of US Marine Corps F4U Corsair squadrons in the Solomons in early 1943 signaled the beginning of the Zero-sen's decline. The Hellcat squadrons of the US Navy's fast carriers forced the Imperial Japanese Navy's Zero-sen units still further onto the defensive, and in a series of clashes during 1943–44 established a level of air superiority that allowed the US Navy to sweep across the Pacific Ocean to the shores of the Philippines and Japan itself.

The dominance the Hellcat achieved in battle against the Zero-sen was also a reflection of the American aviation industry's technological and productive superiority

An F6F-3 Hellcat from VF-16 is cleared for takeoff on board *Lexington* at the start of a mission during November 1943. (80G-471273, RG80, National Archives and Records Service [NARA])

over Japan, especially in respect to airplane engines. This enabled the US Navy to place in combat, in quantity, a second-generation fighter well before the Imperial Japanese Navy Air Force (IJNAF), forcing the latter to continue to rely on the Zero-sen as its principal fighter until the bitter end.

The Hellcat benefited from the American aviation industry's lead over Japan in the development and production of higher power airplane engines. In a post-war memoir Jiro Horikoshi (designer of the Zero-sen) wrote about development of the A6M fighter. He said "of all types of airplanes, none are so dependent upon engine selection as are fighters".

Power is vital to a fighter. The greater the power available, the better the performance, and the greater the load – armament, armor protection, structural strength – that can be carried without sacrificing performance. Most of the first generation of single-engined fighters that fought in the early years of World War II were designed in the mid to late 1930s, when the engines available ranged from 870hp to 1,200hp.

In this period, both the main American engine manufacturers, the Pratt & Whitney Aircraft Company and the Wright Aeronautical Corporation, had air-cooled radial engines generating around 1,000hp. Wright had its nine-cylinder R-1820 Cyclone engine and Pratt & Whitney the two-row 14-cylinder R-1830 Twin Wasp. There was intense competition between the two companies to develop radial engines of even greater power for their commercial and military customers who wanted aircraft with ever better performance. In 1937, Wright Aeronautical introduced the R-2600 Cyclone 14, a 14-cylinder, double-row engine generating 1,500hp that powered the new Boeing Model 314 Clipper. By 1940, Wright had pushed the output of the R-2600 to 1,700hp.

Wright's introduction of the R-2600 forced Pratt & Whitney to abandon its own efforts to develop an engine of similar power and concentrate instead on building an

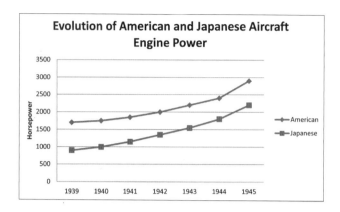

Evolution of American and Japanese Aircraft Engine Power

[Source – T.A.I.C. Summary No 16 "Evolution of Japanese Airplane Engines", November 1944]

engine rated at 1,800hp. This became the 18-cylinder Pratt & Whitney R-2800 Double Wasp that soon generated 2,000hp. Chosen for the Chance Vought F4U, the Republic P-47 and the Martin B-26, the R-2800 was in full production by 1941. By the time that Grumman Aircraft was refining the design that would become the F6F Hellcat, the US Navy had two powerful engines to choose from.

Japan's aviation industry lagged behind America in aircraft engine design. Following World War I, Japanese aviation began a period of intensive development, initially borrowing heavily from foreign designs and employing foreign engineers. In the field of aircraft engines, Japanese firms built several types under license to gain experience. During the 1930s, the two main engine manufacturers, Mitsubishi Jukogyo Kabushiki Kaisha (Mitsubishi Heavy Industries, Ltd) and Nakajima Hikoki Kabushiki Kaisha (Nakajima Aircraft Company) developed and put into production air-cooled radial engines of their own design. When Jiro Horikoshi set about designing the Experimental 12-Shi Carrier-Based Fighter (which evolved into the Zero-sen) in late 1937, he had three engines available – the 875hp Mitsubishi Zuisei 13, the 1,070hp Mitsubishi Kinsei 46 and the 950hp Nakajima Sakae 12. The IJNAF chose the Sakae engine for its new fighter, and versions of the Sakae powered the Zero-sen until the end of the war.

The existence of the powerful Pratt & Whitney R-2800 engines had become public knowledge by early 1940, as had the fact that the US Navy was using this engine in its latest fighter. During this period, it took approximately three years to bring an engine from the experimental stage to full production, assuming there were no complications with the design.

By 1940, both Mitsubishi and Nakajima had developed air-cooled radial engines of around 1,500hp. The IJNAF and the Japanese aviation industry both recognized the urgent need to catch up with American aircraft engine developments. Mitsubishi

A captured A6M5 Model 52 in flight, showing the individual exhaust stacks that identified the Model 52. This airplane was found abandoned on Saipan and returned to the United States for extensive testing against American fighters. (80G-248975, RG80, NARA)

and Nakajima began working on even more powerful 18-cylinder engines aiming at 2,000hp or better, but Japan's lower level of technical and industrial development simply did not allow it to close the gap fast enough. Many of the Japanese designs of this follow-on generation such as the Mitsubishi J2M Raiden ("Jack") and the Kawanishi N1K1 Shiden ("George") encountered technical problems and consequently suffered inordinately long development periods – a reflection of the immature state of the Japanese aviation industry when compared to the West. These aircraft were built in numbers too few to have any real impact on their US opponents. The Mitsubishi A7M Reppu, intended to replace the Zero-sen, suffered even more delays in its development, to the extent that only seven prototypes and one production aircraft had been completed by war's end.

An F6F-3 Hellcat takes off from *Independence* class light carrier USS *Monterey* (CVL-26) for a strike on Saipan during the battle for the Marianas in June 1944. The flightdecks of the CVLs were 35ft narrower than the larger *Essex* class carriers. (80G-468803, RG80, NARA)

Having started on the development of higher powered engines later than the American aviation industry, the problems that naturally emerged did so against a background of engineering staffs stretched almost to breaking point, shortages of skilled labor and the necessary machine tools, and rapidly declining supplies of the critical metals high performance engines required. The IJNAF had no alternative to continuing production of the first-generation A6M Zero-sen. As Japan's situation worsened, the veteran fighter underwent a series of modifications in an attempt to improve its performance, armament and self-protection, but the Mitsubishi machine never managed to catch up with the more powerful Hellcat, which was a generation ahead of the 1937 Zero-sen. As Adm William Moffett, Chief, Bureau of Aeronautics, 1921-33, said, "No airplane is better than its powerplant".

Until the very end of the war, the Zero-sen's lower-powered Sakae engine, relative to the Hellcat's more powerful R-2800, acted as a constraint on its performance. In capable hands, the Zero-sen remained a dangerous foe to any pilot foolish enough to attempt to fight it on its own terms. However, by the time the F6F Hellcat entered combat, US Navy pilots had learned to avoid the close-in maneuvering combat in which the IJNAF fighter excelled, and instead used their greater speed and armament to their advantage in diving attacks from higher altitudes. As the more experienced Japanese fighter pilots were steadily whittled away through constant attrition as the war went on, the duels between the Hellcat and the Zero-sen became evermore one-sided in the Grumman fighter's favor.

CHRONOLOGY

1938

February
Grumman proposes equipping the XF4F-2 with the new Wright R-2600 engine as the Model G-35.

October
The US Navy awards Grumman a contract for the XF4F-3.

1939

April 1
Mitsubishi Experimental 12-Shi Carrier Fighter makes its first flight.

August
US Navy awards Grumman a contract for 54 F4F-3 fighters.

1940

May 29
Chance Vought XF4U makes its first flight with a Pratt & Whitney R-2800 engine.

July
Operational debut of the Mitsubishi A6M1 Zero-sen over China.

September
Grumman continues work on its improved Wildcat, fitted with the Wright R-2600 engine, as the Model G-50.

1941

June
US Navy orders two prototypes of the Grumman G-50 as the XF6F-1.

1942

January 7
US Navy signs a production contract for 1,080 F6F-1 aircraft.

April
A6M3 Model 32 Zero-sen becomes operational.

June 26
XF6F-1 makes its first flight with Wright R-2600 engine.

July 30
Revised XF6F-3, fitted with a more powerful Pratt & Whitney R-2800 engine, makes its first flight.

October 3
First production F6F-3 makes its first flight.

1943

January
VF-9 becomes the first US Navy squadron to convert to the F6F-3.

August
Mitsubishi begins production of the A6M5 Model 52 Zero-sen.

September 6
Ens James Warren of VF-33, based at Guadalcanal, becomes the first Hellcat pilot to claim a Zero-sen in aerial combat.

A6M2 Model 21 Zero-sens at an airfield on Rabaul in 1942. The first model produced in quantity, the A6M2 equipped the IJNAF's carrier and land-based air groups until replaced by newer models toward the end of 1942. (via the author)

The F6F-3 production line at Grumman's Bethpage, New York, factory in February 1943. The company built just 35 Hellcats that month, but in December of that year it produced 458 examples and through 1944 Grumman was churning out an average of 500+ F6Fs per month. (80G-35834, RG80, NARA)

October 5	First combat between carrier-borne Hellcats and Zero-sens takes place over Wake Island.
November 5	Carrier strike on Rabaul.
December 4	Carrier strike on Kwajalein.

1944

February 17	Carrier strike on the Japanese bastion at Truk. Hellcat squadrons claim more than 80 Zero-sens shot down.
March	Mitsubishi and Nakajima begin production of the A6M5a Model 52a Zero-sen.
April	Mitsubishi and Nakajima begin production of the A6M5b Model 52b Zero-sen for Operation *A-Go*.
April	Grumman begins production of the improved F6F-5 Hellcat.
June 19	Hellcat pilots take part in the "Great Marianas Turkey Shoot" during the First Battle of the Philippine Sea, claiming 346 IJNAF aircraft shot down in a single day.

September	Nakajima begins production of the A6M5c Model 52c Zero-sen.
October 20	US Navy carriers support the liberation of the Philippines, which commences with amphibious landings on the island of Leyte.
November	A6M6c prototype flies, with subsequent production assigned to Nakajima.

Grumman switched to producing the F6F-5 in early April 1944, the "Dash Five" incorporating a number of refinements tested on the F6F-3 and F6F-3N. With the R-2800-10W engine, which used water injection, the F6F-5 had a maximum speed of 380mph. (80G-228822, RG80, NARA)

DESIGN AND DEVELOPMENT

F6F HELLCAT

The genesis of the F6F Hellcat dates back to discussions the Grumman Aircraft Engineering Corporation had with the US Navy's Bureau of Aeronautics in early 1938. At the time, Grumman was heavily involved in testing its new XF4F-2 monoplane fighter for the US Navy. The XF4F-2's 1,050hp Pratt & Whitney R-1830-66 engine with a single-stage supercharger gave it a maximum speed of around 290mph. At a conference between Grumman engineers and Bureau of Aeronautics representatives in January 1938, there was a discussion about modifying the XF4F-2 to take the new and more powerful 1,600hp Wright R-2600 engine. The Bureau indicated it might decide to place a contract with Grumman for an experimental fighter with the Wright engine, if the desired maximum and landing speeds could be obtained.

In February, Leroy Grumman sent an informal proposal to the Bureau stating that Grumman could provide a prototype of a modified XF4F-2 within 120 days. Grumman engineers estimated that the modified airplane with the R-2600 would have a maximum speed of 320mph, with the stalling speed of 70mph the US Navy required. Grumman engineers believed that modifying the XF4F-2 to take the R-2600 "has practically no effect on the external dimensions and appearance of the XF4F-2 airplane". Grumman proposed that the new airplane, the Model G-33, should retain the XF4F-2's mid-wing design, with an increase in fuel capacity and the same armament of one 0.30in. and one 0.50in. machine gun in the nose, with provision for two more 0.50in. machine guns in the wing.

The Bureau of Aeronautics was less sanguine about Grumman's ability to adopt the Wright engine to the XF4F-2 without major modifications. The Bureau believed the increase in gross weight from the heavier engine would push the landing speed above acceptable limits, thus necessitating the creation of a new wing design, and alter the center of gravity unfavorably. It also felt that the larger propeller needed to absorb the greater power of the Wright engine would reduce the ground clearance below the US Navy's requirements with the XF4F-2's landing gear configuration. Instead, for its 1938 fighter design competition the US Navy chose to pursue the Grumman XF5F-1, its first twin-engined fighter, over a more powerful XF4F-2.

In this same competition, the US Navy gave a contract to Chance Vought for the XF4U-1 with the new Pratt & Whitney R-2800 engine. But neither Grumman nor the US Navy gave up completely on the idea of a more powerful version of the XF4F, even after the former won a contract for production of the revised F4F-3.

In September 1940, Grumman submitted a revised design to the Bureau of Aeronautics as the Model G-50. This was an improved version of the F4F with a Wright R-2600-10 engine, using a two-stage supercharger, providing 1,700hp at takeoff. At this stage the Model G-50 looked like a larger F4F. Grumman had increased the wingspan by approximately four feet by adding two-foot-wide wing stubs between the F4F's wing and the fuselage, and lengthened the fuselage by two feet, but retained the fuselage-mounted landing gear. Grumman estimated that the Model G-50 would have a top speed of close to 380mph.

Although the Bureau of Aeronautics thought the Model G-50 was an attractive design, it was still not satisfied with the airplane's balance and center of gravity. In addition, the Bureau pointed out to Grumman that "recent developments have led to additional requirements for Class VF aircraft which must be met if the airplane in question is to be considered satisfactory for service use".

Based on reports coming in from US Navy observers in Europe, the Bureau of Aeronautics realized that it needed carrier fighters with higher speed, greater range, heavier armament and more armor protection. The Bureau now wanted a maximum speed of close to 400mph, a range of 1,500 miles with on-board and droppable fuel tanks, armament of six 0.50in. machine guns with 400 rounds per gun or four 20mm cannon with 120 rounds per gun, and protection for the pilot, fuel tanks and oil tank. To maximize the number of aircraft on its carriers, the Bureau mandated folding wing mechanisms. Looking at a range of fighter designs employing both air-cooled and liquid-cooled engines, the Bureau thought it would be desirable to have other air-cooled radial engine designs as competition for the Chance Vought F4U. A redesign of the F4F held promise, particularly if Grumman could explore the possibility of housing the landing gear in the wing instead of the fuselage. The Bureau requested that Grumman modify its design and resubmit its proposal in light of these new requirements.

Grumman engineers went back to their Model G-50 design and, under the leadership of chief engineer William T. Schwendler, made a number of significant modifications. The design team abandoned the traditional Grumman fuselage-mounted landing gear and replaced it with a revised wide landing gear built into the wing stubs that retracted

OVERLEAF
This F6F-3 Hellcat is representative of the thousands of Grumman fighters that served on the US Navy's fast carriers during the Pacific War. Serving with VF-1 aboard *Yorktown*, this aircraft was hit by anti-aircraft fire during strikes against the Marianas in June 1944 and suffered further damage when landing back aboard the carrier. Judged to be beyond the vessel's basic repair capabilities, the deck crew promptly pushed the Hellcat over the side. With Grumman producing hundreds of Hellcats each month, and with a reliable and speedy flow of replacement aircraft to the fleet, it was simply more practical to dump a damaged airplane into the ocean and replace it with a new one, rather than attempt the repairs aboard the carrier. The turnover of aircraft in a squadron was constant as Hellcats were damaged and discarded, or flown back to island bases for more extensive servicing after reaching a certain number of flying hours. It was not uncommon for a pilot to fly two- or three-dozen different Hellcats during the course of a single combat cruise.

F6F-3 HELLCAT

33ft 7in.

42ft 10in.

to the rear. This change enabled the fighter to take a larger diameter propeller. The Model G-50 changed from a mid-wing design similar to the F4F to a new low-wing configuration. Good vision forward and downward for the pilot had been one of the new requirements the Bureau of Aeronautics requested in its discussions with Grumman. The G-50 design placed the cockpit high above the low wing and had the nose of the fighter slope downward, giving the pilot excellent forward visibility.

In January 1941 the US Navy inspected a mock-up of the revised design and requested two changes. The fuselage was lengthened by 26 inches and the wing area increased from 290 square feet to 334 square feet to accommodate more fuel, ammunition and armor protection for the wing guns. The final design bore little resemblance to the F4F, being substantially larger and heavier. On June 19, 1941 the US Navy ordered two prototypes (designated XF6F-1s) from Grumman to be powered by the 1,700hp Wright R-2600-10 engine. A month after the attack on Pearl Harbor, with the nation now at war, the US Navy placed a production order with Grumman for 1,080 F6F-1s with Wright engines.

The XF6F-1 made its first flight on June 26, 1942, with Grumman test pilot Robert Hall at the controls. The flight revealed some minor problems centering on excessive trim changes and longitudinal stability. On a more serious note, Grumman found that the prototype did not meet all the US Navy's performance requirements, particularly in respect to speed and rate of climb. Fortunately, a solution was already in the works. While revising the G-50 design, Grumman engineers had considered the possibility of switching from the Wright R-2600-10 to the more powerful Pratt & Whitney R-2800 engine, and had designed the XF6F-1 so that it could take the larger 18-cylinder engine if necessary.

From initial combat experience in the first few months of the Pacific War, the US Navy decided that even more power would be needed in its new fighter. Grumman was duly instructed to equip the second XF6F-1 with the R-2800-10 engine and a Curtiss Electric propeller and spinner. The modified prototype was designated the XF6F-3, and the aircraft made its first flight a little over a month after the XF6F-1, on July 30, 1942. Grumman and the US Navy knew that they had a winner.

The Grumman XF6F-1 prototype around the time of its first flight on June 26, 1942. The XF6F-1 was fitted with the 1,700hp Wright R-2600 Cyclone engine, but with this powerplant the fighter did not meet the US Navy's performance expectations. (72-AC-21G-10, RG72, NARA)

13

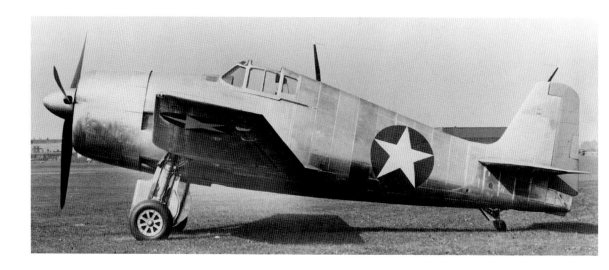

The Grumman XF6F-3 with the larger Pratt & Whitney Double Wasp R-2800 engine. Note the lengthened cowl to cover the larger engine. With the more powerful R-2800, the F6F-3 had a maximum speed of around 375mph at 17,000ft. (80G-34229, RG80, NARA)

An early production F6F-3 in flight. Grumman had the first production examples of the F6F-3 flying a little over three months after the first flight of the XF6F-1 – a remarkable achievement. (Robert Lawson Collection, National Naval Aviation Museum)

Remarkably, the first production F6F-3 made its first flight on October 3, 1942 – a little over three months after the first flight of the prototype XF6F-1. So that Grumman could concentrate on production of the Hellcat and the development of follow-on fighter designs, the US Navy transferred production of the F4F Wildcat and the TBF Avenger to the Eastern Aircraft Division of General Motors as the FM-1/FM-2 and TBM. There were only a few modifications needed to turn the XF6F-3 into the production model F6F-3. The covers for the undercarriage were simplified, the propeller spinner removed and the propeller changed to a Hamilton Standard Hydromatic constant-speed unit.

In January 1943 VF-9 became the first US Navy squadron to receive the F6F-3 Hellcat, with other fleet fighter squadrons converting as rapidly as Grumman could expand production. By early July the US Navy had 263 Hellcats on strength distributed among 13 squadrons, which were either fully equipped or converting to the new Grumman fighter.

The F6F-3 Hellcat could not have arrived at a more opportune, or critical, time. The US Navy had found to its disappointment that the F4U-1 Corsair, despite outstanding

performance at altitude, had less than desirable deck-landing qualities, with limited visibility over the nose and poor stalling characteristics at low speeds. The US Navy decided that the Corsair would not be suitable as a carrier fighter just as the new *Essex* class fleet carriers and the smaller *Independence* class vessels were coming into service. The new carrier air groups the US Navy was forming for its growing carrier force badly needed a new, more capable, fighter to gain air superiority over the Zero-sen, clearing the sky for the dive-bombers and torpedo-bombers that comprised the carrier strike force, and to defend the carriers from air attack.

By great good fortune the Hellcat became available when it was most needed, and proved to be not only far easier to land on a carrier than the Corsair – an important consideration for the many young Naval Aviators fresh out of training – but also to have the performance to overcome the Zero-sen.

In April 1944, having completed 4,402 F6F-3 airplanes, Grumman shifted to building the F6F-5, the second production model of the Hellcat. There was no prototype for the F6F-5. Grumman simply shifted production from one model to the other, completing the first F6F-5 on April 4 and the last F6F-3 on April 21. The F6F-5 incorporated a number of minor modifications to improve speed, visibility and versatility based on extensive testing of the F6F-3 and reports from combat pilots in the Pacific. Grumman would complete 7,868 F6F-5 Hellcats before the end of the war.

The F6F-5 was powered by the Pratt & Whitney R-2800-10W engine, its water-menthol injection allowing the motor to produce 2,200hp at emergency power and 1,650hp at 22,000ft. A redesigned and more streamlined engine cowling gave the "Dash Five" model a higher maximum speed and a better rate of climb than the F6F-3. In response to pilot complaints, Grumman added spring tabs to the F6F-5's ailerons to improve the rate of roll at speeds above 200mph. To improve forward visibility, the F6F-5 featured a revised front windshield with a flat armored glass plate. A change in the armament configuration allowed the substitution of 20mm cannon for the inboard 0.50in. guns – a feature adopted on many of the F6F-5N nightfighters produced.

Hellcat squadrons in the Pacific had begun using the F6F-3 as a fighter-bomber during the early months of 1944. The F6F-5 featured improvements to enable the

The US Navy tested an armament of four 20mm cannon on the XF6F-4, but adopted a battery of six 0.50in. Browning M-2 machine guns as standard for the F6F-3. With 400 rounds per gun, this proved more than adequate against the more lightly built and poorly armored Zero-sen. (72-AC-21H-2, RG72, NARA)

airplane to carry a heavier ordnance load. A Mk 51 bomb rack was added under the inboard section of each wing stub, and this was capable of carrying a 1,000lb bomb or a drop tank. Three Mk 5 zero-length rocket launchers were fitted to the outer wing section to carry five-inch High-Velocity Aircraft Rockets (HVARs).

When the Japanese introduced kamikaze attacks during the Philippines campaign in late 1944, the US Navy responded by increasing the number of fighters embarked in the larger *Essex* class carriers to 72. These machines were split into separate fighter (VF) and fighter-bomber (VBF) squadrons, space for the additional F6Fs and F4Us being found after a significant number of TBM Avengers and SB2C Helldivers were removed from the carriers. Hellcats and Corsairs of the VBF squadrons subsequently took over more of the attack missions.

The F6F-5 improved the margin of performance the F6F-3 Hellcat had over the Zero-sen. Tests against a captured A6M5 in October 1944 showed that the Model 52 had a better rate of climb than the Hellcat up to 9,000ft, after which the Zero-sen's advantage gradually declined. Above 14,000ft, the Hellcat had the advantage in rate of climb. The F6F-5 proved to be faster than the A6M5 at all altitudes, as the flight test report noted:

- At sea level the F6F-5 was 41mph faster than the Zeke 52.
- At 5,000ft the F6F-5 was 41mph faster than the Zeke 52.
- At 10,000ft the F6F-5 was 45mph faster than the Zeke 52.
- At 15,000ft the F6F-5 was 62mph faster than the Zeke 52.
- At 20,000ft the F6F-5 was 69mph faster than the Zeke 52.
- At 25,000ft the F6F-5 was 75mph faster than the Zeke 52.

Only in turns and maneuverability at speeds below 175 knots did the A6M5 retain its advantage, being judged far superior to the F6F-5, although the Zero-sen's advantage declined significantly at higher speeds. Still, the flight test report ended with the admonition "DO NOT DOGFIGHT WITH THE ZEKE 52".

A6M ZERO-SEN

As described in *Osprey Duel 54 – F4F Wildcat vs A6M Zero-sen*, Jiro Horikoshi and his design team accomplished the seemingly impossible task of meeting the IJNAF's demanding specifications for its Experimental 12-Shi Carrier Fighter that became the A6M Zero-sen. Indeed, his design boasted the required speed, range, maneuverability and armament, the fighter's 14-cylinder Nakajima Sakae 13 engine of 950hp powering a superbly designed lightweight airplane.

At the time of its operational debut in China during the summer of 1940, the A6M2 was without question the finest carrier fighter in the world. Within a few months Zero-sen pilots would claim 59 aerial victories over China without a single loss. Even with this exceptional record, and their delight with their new fighter, IJNAF pilots complained about certain aspects of the Zero-sen's performance – specifically a lack of adequate aileron control at higher speeds. This was the first indication of certain inherent weaknesses in the Zero-sen's design that would emerge when the aircraft was forced to combat a new and more powerful generation of American fighters.

In its requirements for the Experimental 12-Shi Carrier Fighter the IJNAF had stressed the importance of maneuverability. Fighter pilots wanted an airplane with an exceptionally short turning radius and excellent roll rates at low speeds to excel at dogfighting and to ease takeoffs and landings on carrier decks. To achieve these goals, Horikoshi and his team chose a large wing area and low wing loading for the new fighter, with large ailerons for better roll rates, realizing that this choice would compromise the fighter's diving and level speeds, and lateral maneuverability as speeds increased. But maneuverability remained paramount.

In comparative trials with the Japanese Army Air Force's Nakajima Type 97 fighter ("Nate"), Type 1 Fighter Hayabusa ("Oscar"), Type 2 Fighter Shoki ("Tojo") and an imported Heinkel He 100, conducted in January 1941, the A6M2 Zero-sen demonstrated its superiority in dogfighting. The He 100 proved to be faster than the Zero-sen in level flight, but the IJNAF did not think steps to increase the Mitsubishi's speed were worth the cost of the resultant loss of maneuverability. While exceptional maneuverability at low speeds remained the Zero-sen's main advantage over its

The A6M3 Model 32 succeeded the A6M2 Model 21, although its performance was less than Mitsubishi and the IJNAF had hoped for. Despite the Model 32 being fitted with the more powerful Sakae 21 engine of 1,150 hp, it was only marginally faster than the Model 21. Note that the Japanese censor has removed any sign of unit markings from this photograph. (via the author)

With its heavier engine and reduced fuel capacity, the A6M3 Model 32 lacked the range of its predecessor. As a result the aircraft could not reach Guadalcanal from bases at Rabaul. Mitsubishi hurriedly developed the A6M3 Model 22, restoring the longer wings of the Model 21 and adding more fuel capacity to give the Model 22 the longest range of any Zero-sen. (Jack Lambert Collection, Museum of Flight)

American rivals, the A6M began to lag behind in performance at altitude, maneuverability at higher speeds, armament and protection for airplane and the pilot.

The complaints and recommendations Mitsubishi and the IJNAF received were a source of motivation for implementing a series of improvements to the Zero-sen. By early 1941 it was apparent that Japan's probable enemies were producing engines and aircraft of increasing performance. Indeed, the 1940 edition of *Jane's All the World's Aircraft* listed the maximum speed of the Supermarine Spitfire as 367mph and the Lockheed P-38 as 404mph, while articles appearing in the American aviation press in the fall of 1940 made mention of the 1,850hp Pratt & Whitney Double Wasp engine. The IJNAF and Mitsubishi sought ways of improving the Zero-sen's speed and rate of climb, and responding to the need for greater aileron control at higher speeds.

The Nakajima Aircraft Company had been working on a more powerful version of their Sakae engine incorporating a two-stage supercharger. This engine, designated the Sakae 21, offered 1,130hp for takeoff, 1,100hp at 9,350ft, and 980hp at

The arrival of the Vought F4U Corsair in the Solomons in February 1943 presented a serious challenge to the Zero-sen pilots flying the A6M3 from Rabaul and Bougainville, prompting calls for urgent improvement of the fighter's performance. (Museum of Flight)

19,685ft – a measurable improvement over the Sakae 12. Mitsubishi adapted the Sakae 21 to the Zero-sen, designing a new cowling to accommodate the larger engine. Due to the Sakae 21's increased size and weight, the fuselage fuel tank had to be reduced from 26 to 16 gallons. This had an adverse effect on range, as the Sakae 21 had higher fuel consumption than the Sakae 12. The IJNAF instructed Mitsubishi to remove the folding wing mechanisms from the new model, squaring off the wingtips and reducing the wingspan to 11 meters (36ft). This improved the rate of roll at higher speeds. At the request of units in the field, the ammunition supply for the two 20mm wing cannon was increased to 100 rounds per gun.

The new model was designated the A6M3 Model 32, and after successful test flights it was put into production, entering operational service in April 1942. To the disappointment of Mitsubishi, despite its more powerful engine, the performance of the A6M3 was not significantly greater than the earlier A6M2, the newer Model 32 having only a modest increase in maximum speed. Surprisingly, despite

The A6M5 Model 52 was designed in response to requests for improved performance. Two of its key features are shown here, namely the individual exhaust stacks that boosted maximum speed to 351mph at 19,000 ft, and the longer barrel Type 99-2 20mm cannon that fired a more powerful cartridge with a higher muzzle velocity. (80G-169292, RG80, NARA)

reports from the air war in Europe indicating the need for greater protection for the pilot and fuel tanks, the IJNAF did not address these needs in the A6M3.

In the late spring of 1942 the A6M3 Model 32 entered combat in the skies over New Guinea. Following the American landings on Guadalcanal in August, A6M3s of the 2nd Kokutai transferred to Buka Island, north of Bougainville, and were thrown into the violent aerial battles over Henderson Field. The Model 32's shorter range contributed to higher operational losses, leading units in the Solomons to demand an increase in fuel capacity. Mitsubishi restored the longer wing of the A6M2 and added additional fuel tanks to create the A6M3 Model 22, which had the greatest range of any Zero-sen model. With the earlier A6M2 Model 21, the Model 32 and the Model 22 bore the brunt of the fighting over the Solomon Islands during the latter months of 1942 and well into 1943 against US Navy and US Marine Corps F4F-4s and US Army Air Force P-39s and P-40s. In November 1942, the P-38 made its combat debut, followed by the F4U Corsair (the first Allied single-engined fighter to present a serious challenge to the Zero-sen) in February 1943.

In early April 1943, during a conference held at Rabaul with Adm Isoroku Yamamoto, Commander-in-Chief of the IJN's Combined Fleet, senior air staff officers presented their conclusion that the Zero-sen was still an excellent fighter airplane. In their view, American fighters had yet to undermine the Zero-sen's capabilities – a remarkably complacent conclusion given the arrival of the F4U Corsair in growing numbers. However, the conference noted the pronounced change in enemy tactics. Whenever possible American pilots avoided close-in dogfighting with the Zero-sen and resorted to high-speed diving attacks and deflection shooting. The newer P-38 and F4Us were a challenge as they used their superior altitude performance and higher speeds to mount slashing attacks that the Zero-sen pilots were struggling to counter. Finally, because the lightweight Zero-sen was slower than its heavier Allied counterparts in a dive, IJNAF pilots were hampered in their ability to pursue enemy fighters as they broke away after conducting a slashing attack.

Because the opportunities to engage enemy fighters had become more fleeting, Zero-sen pilots wanted additional cannon fitted in their fighters, more ammunition per gun and a faster rate of fire. Belatedly, the operational units now wanted more protection for the pilot and the fuel tanks, noting that in many aerial battles half the Zero-sens lost went down in flames. Many of these recommendations were incorporated in the newer fighter models then under development in Japan, principally the J2M Raiden and the N1K1 Shiden, but their entry into service was well-behind schedule. The failure to introduce the next generation of fighters during 1943 left the IJNAF with no choice but to demand that Mitsubishi work to improve the performance of the Zero-sen.

The manufacturer had by then transferred responsibility for further development of the Zero-sen to Mijiro Takahashi so that Jiro Horikoshi could concentrate on the 14-Shi Interceptor Fighter (the J2M Raiden) and the badly delayed 17-Shi Experimental Carrier Fighter, the latter intended as a replacement for the A6M series. In the summer of 1943, Takahashi and his team worked up several modifications to the A6M3 Model 32 to improve its maximum and diving speeds and armament. They retained the shorter wingspan of the Model 32, but rounded off the fighter's wingtips and increased the thickness of the wing skinning to allow for an increase in the maximum diving speed to 410mph.

The modified Zero-sen, designated the A6M5 Model 52, retained the Sakae 21 engine, but incorporated individual exhaust stacks for thrust augmentation, pushing the top speed to 351mph at 19,685ft. The Model 52 kept the twin nose-mounted 7.7mm machine guns of the A6M3, but changed the 20mm cannon to the longer barrel Type 99-2, which had a higher muzzle velocity than the Type 99-1, although at the cost of a lower rate of fire – in some ways a retrograde step. The A6M5 Model 52 went into production in August 1943, just as the Zero-sen was about to encounter its most formidable opponent.

Although the first clashes between the Zero-sen and the F6F took place in the Solomons, the US Navy's newest fighter does not seem to have made as dramatic an impression there as it did during the first combats between carrier-borne Hellcats and the Zero-sen units defending Japan's island bases in the Central Pacific. On October 5, 1943, Hellcats from USS *Essex* (CV-9), USS *Yorktown* (CV-10), USS *Lexington* (CV-16) and USS *Cowpens* (CVL-25), which were all part of Task Force 14,

A6M5 ZERO-SEN MODEL 52

29ft 11in.

11ft 6in.

36ft 1in.

clashed with 23 Zero-sens from the 252nd Kokutai over Wake Island, shooting down 16 IJNAF machines. A short time later more Hellcats downed three out of seven Zero-sens escorting a force of Navy Type 1 Attack Bombers.

For Ens Isamu Miazaki, an experienced Zero-sen pilot who survived both this encounter and the war, the combat marked the moment when the myth of the Zero-sen's invincibility collapsed. The Hellcat attack, he recalled after the war, was "like a hurricane". In his post-war memoir Jiro Horikoshi recalled his feeling on learning of the performance of the new Hellcat. "A fighter that could fight straight in the Zero's face had finally appeared in the United States' arsenal".

It was not simply that the Hellcat was faster than the Zero-sen and could, therefore, easily pull away from the Japanese fighter. The Hellcat had the lowest wing loading of any of the second-generation American fighters, and as a result could follow the Zero-sen in certain maneuvers, especially at higher speeds where the Mitsubishi's controls stiffened markedly. While the Zero-sen remained supremely maneuverable at low speeds, its margin of superiority was clearly diminished. Zero-sen pilots were also astonished at the Hellcat's ability to take punishment. Their 7.7mm machine gun fire seemed to barely penetrate the skin of the American fighter, and even six 20mm shells – about all a skilled pilot could get off in a rapid encounter – were not always enough to bring down the big Grumman fighter.

The calls for improvements to the Zero-sen became incessant, but Mitsubishi could only respond with what were stopgap measures. In the A6M5a, A6M5b, and A6M5c, Mitsubishi made modifications to the wing skinning to increase the diving speed, added protection for the pilot and the fuel tanks and gradually changed the armament over to a combination of 20mm cannon and more rapid firing 13.2mm machine guns. Although the A6M5 was still faster than the A6M3, these modifications added several hundred pounds to it, causing pilots to complain that the Zero-sen had lost some of its excellent flying qualities.

Mitsubishi's preferred solution to regaining a better balance of performance against the Hellcat was to replace the 1,130hp Sakae engine with the newer Kinsei motor that now generated 1,500hp, but the IJNAF adamantly refused. Desperate for more fighters to make up for heavy attrition, the IJNAF had no interest in any modification that, no matter how desperately needed, might have interrupted production of the Zero-sen. It stuck to this position until the final months of the Pacific War, by which time it was far too late.

TECHNICAL SPECIFICATIONS

The F6F-3 was the first production model of the Hellcat, Grumman building 4,402 examples between October 1942 and April 1944. The US Navy developed two nightfighter versions of the "Dash Three", the F6F-3E with the AN/APS-4 radar, and the F6F-3N with the AN/APS-6. Several improvements developed for the F6F-3N went into the F6F-5. This F6F-3 served with VF-16 when the unit was embarked in *Lexington*. (Robert Lawson Collection, National Naval Aviation Museum)

F6F HELLCAT

F6F-3

The Hellcat was a large airplane, taller, longer, with a greater wingspan and some 60 percent heavier than its predecessor, the F4F Wildcat. During its production life the F6F Hellcat went through only minor modifications. The F6F-3, the first production model, differed from the prototype XF6F-3 in deleting the propeller spinner, substituting a Hamilton Standard propeller instead of the Curtiss Electric model and boasting simplified landing gear fairings.

The Hellcat was built in four sections – nose, fuselage, empennage and wing assembly. The nose section held the engine mounting frame for the Pratt & Whitney R-2800-10 engine and auxiliary equipment. The fuselage

structure was of all-metal, stressed skin semi-monocoque construction built up from flanged ring fuselage frames, with aluminum longerons running the length of the fuselage to provide longitudinal support. An aluminum alloy skinning was flush-riveted over this framework. The fuselage was bolted to the wing center section, with the cockpit placed high over the latter so as to give the pilot the best possible visibility over the nose. The empennage was built of metal and attached to the rear of the fuselage assembly. The rudder and elevators were built out of aluminum framing and were fabric covered. The empennage housed the retractable tail wheel and tail hook.

The wing assembly came in five sections and was mounted in a low-mid position on the fuselage. The center section, attached directly to the fuselage, held the two main fuel tanks. Two stub sections, attached to either side of the center section, housed the rearward-retracting landing gear and the attachment points for the folding outer wing sections. The detachable outer wing sections contained the Hellcat's armament and could be folded manually aft alongside the fuselage. When spread forward, the outer wing sections were locked in place with hydraulically operated locking pins that the pilot controlled. The wing center section was built around two cantilever beams, with the wing-fold mechanism attaching to the front beam. The wing stubs and the outer wing sections continued the two beam structure, with a third beam to the rear for the attachment of the ailerons and flap assemblies. The beams, ribs and bulkheads

The F6F Hellcat was renowned for its ruggedness. This F6F-3 of VF-1 was damaged in combat over the Marianas during the June 1944 battles and lost its tail landing back aboard Yorktown. Hellcats regularly brought their pilots back to the carriers despite being heavily damaged. (80G-474473, RG80, NARA)

were all of metal construction, while the ailerons and outboard flaps were fabric over metal framing.

Apart from its more powerful engine and greater size and strength, where the Hellcat differed markedly from the Zero-sen was in its armament and armor protection. While the US Navy had considered installing four 20mm cannon, it chose a battery of six 0.50in. machine guns as the standard armament of its new fighters, the XF4U and the XF6F, and the F4F-4 version of the Wildcat. Although the 0.50in. machine gun was not as powerful a weapon as the 20mm cannon, the Browning M-2 was highly reliable. Furthermore, standardization with the other American military services allowed for greater rates of production and simpler logistics. The Browning M-2 fired a cartridge with a higher muzzle velocity than the 20mm round of the Zero-sen's Type 99-2 cannon, giving long range and a penetrative power more than adequate for

F6F-3/5 HELLCAT MACHINE GUNS

The Hellcat's six 0.50in. Browning M-2 machine guns were mounted in the outer wing sections and were staggered to ease the ammunition feed to the guns and storage for the metal ammunition boxes. The latter contained 400 rounds per gun, a welcome increase from the F4F-4 Wildcat's approximately 240 rounds per gun. The weapons could be reloaded from underneath the wing when the outer wings were folded up against the fuselage. The gun compartments were heated electrically, and the guns charged by the pilot with charging handles in the cockpit. A Mk 8 electric gunsight was mounted on the combing above the instrument panel.

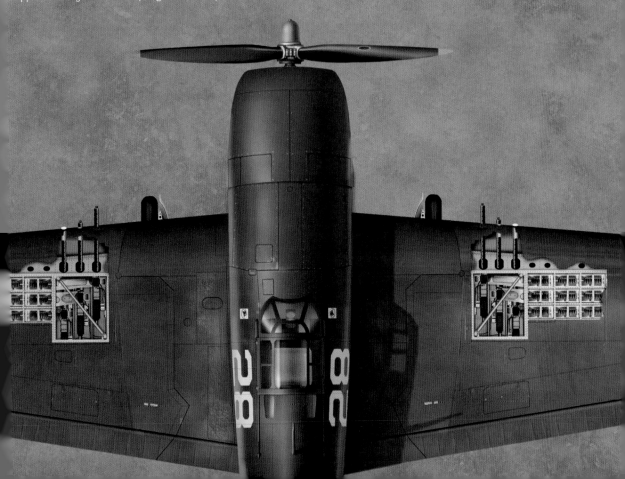

The F6F-5 featured a more streamlined cowling for an increase in maximum speed and hard points under each wing for three HVARs. Later production models of the F6F-5 dispensed with the side windows behind the cockpit. Here, crewmen attach rockets to the hard points of an F6F-5 from VF-80 assigned to strike targets in the Philippine capital, Manila, in late 1944. (80G-299903, RG80, NARA)

the lighter built Japanese airplanes. The M-2 also had a higher rate of fire than the Type 99-2. The battery of six 0.50in. machine guns gave Hellcat pilots the added benefit of not having to cope with different shell trajectories.

The Hellcat had extensive protection for the pilot, fuel and oil. The pilot's headrest was attached to a face-hardened sheet of armor plate to protect the pilot's head and shoulders. To guard against attacks from the front a sheet of armor plate was fitted just ahead of the instrument panel, and a sheet of bullet-resistant glass placed in the windscreen. The two 87-gallon fuel tanks in the center wing section were both self-sealing, as was the 60-gallon fuel tank under the cockpit. The 19-gallon oil tank located behind the engine had a section of armor plate in front of the tank for protection against head-on attacks. Another sheet of armor plate protected the oil cooler in front of the R-2800 engine.

F6F-5

The F6F-5 Hellcat incorporated modifications tested on the F6F-3. In the late production models of the "Dash Three", Grumman switched to the 2,200hp R-2800-10W engine. With water injection, the -10W version gave a useful boost in military power. This engine became standard on the F6F-5. A redesigned and more streamlined cowl over the engine helped boost the top speed of the F6F-5 to 380mph at 23,400ft. To improve maneuverability at high speeds, where the Hellcat's controls tightened up, Grumman added spring tabs to the ailerons, making the left hand aileron tab adjustable from the cockpit. Following tests on an F6F-3, Grumman strengthened the rear fuselage structure and the horizontal stabilizers to correct some weakness that had appeared on the "Dash Three" and incorporated these changes into the F6F-5, allowing pilots of the latter fighter to dive at higher speeds and make more violent pull-outs in combat.

The F6F-5 featured several changes in armament. Carrier squadrons in the Pacific had begun using the F6F-3 as a fighter-bomber, with a bomb adapter on the right wing stub capable of carrying a weapon of up to 1,000lb in weight – the aircraft also had provision for a centerline fuel tank. The F6F-5 had fittings for bomb racks beneath both of the wing stubs, these also being cleared for the carriage of 1,000lb bombs. The fighter retained plumbing for the centerline fuel tank. Three Mk 5 Zero Length rocket launchers were attached to each of the outer wings of the F6F-5, allowing six 5in. HVAR rockets to be carried along with the bomb load. This made the Hellcat even more effective in the fighter-bomber role.

Grumman and the US Navy had also experimented with the fitment of four 20mm cannon in the Hellcat in lieu of the six 0.50in. machine guns installed in the XF6F-4. Although this arrangement proved workable, the US Navy decided to maintain the 0.50in. machine guns as the main armament of the F6F-5, but made provision for a 20mm cannon to be substituted for the innermost machine gun in each wing. This became the standard armament for the F6F-5N – the dedicated nightfighter version of the Hellcat.

There were several improvements in the cockpit area incorporating changes developed for the F6F-3N. The F6F-5 featured red lighting for the instrument panel for improved night flying, a modified windscreen with a flat bullet-resistant glass panel and elimination of the two metal braces on the F6F-3 for better visibility, and a larger sheet of armor plate placed just behind the pilot's seat. This provided improved protection from attacks from the rear across a roughly 40-degree span in a horizontal plane and a 25-degree span vertically. Rearward visibility was one problem never resolved on the Hellcat, however. The first 1,000 or so production models of the F6F-5 retained the two side windows aft of the cockpit, but in subsequent airplanes these were removed. Grumman tested a free-blown canopy for the Hellcat that proved successful at moderate speeds, but on a later test flight the canopy disintegrated when the Hellcat was flying at 200mph, and the effort was apparently abandoned.

A6M ZERO-SEN

A6M3 MODEL 32

The A6M Zero-sen retained its basic structure throughout its production life, the major differences among models being the wing shape and span. The Model 32 was the first attempt to improve certain aspects of the Zero-sen's performance. Mitsubishi and the IJNAF had wanted to increase the Zero-sen's performance at altitude, while experience in flight tests and on operations had demonstrated that the fighter's lateral control declined at higher speeds – above 230mph it became more difficult to roll the Zero-sen as the controls tightened up considerably. For better performance at altitude in particular, and overall, Mitsubishi replaced the Nakajima Sakae 12 engine with the

The A6M3 Model 22 was a hurried response to urgent requests from the field to restore the Zero-sen's range so as to enable the new model to reach Guadalcanal from Japanese bases in Rabaul. These aircraft were assigned to the 251st Kokutai at Rabaul, and were photographed here heading out on a patrol in 1943. Each machine is equipped with a 330-liter drop tank. (via Aerospace Publishing)

This A6M5 Model 52 was one of a group of six airplanes captured on Saipan in mid-1944 and returned to the United States for testing and evaluation. The US Navy used one airworthy example for extensive tests against the F6F-5 Hellcat, the F4U-1 Corsair and the FM-2 in the fall of 1944. (80G-307726, RG80, NARA)

more powerful Sakae 21, which had a two-stage supercharger giving an additional 120hp at 19,685ft.

In order to accommodate the larger Sakae 21 and allow the engine's carburetor intake to be moved from the bottom to the top of the powerplant, Mitsubishi revised the shape of the cowl. The first few models of the A6M3 retained the wing of the earlier A6M2, but pilots recommended doing away with the latter's folding wing mechanism in order to save weight. Mitsubishi engineers found that removing a little over three feet from the wingspan, squaring off the wingtips and reducing the length of the ailerons by about one foot provided better lateral control and roll performance for a minor loss in rate of climb and turn radius. Interestingly, Allied examination of captured Model 32s revealed that

although the wing had been squared off, the locking and folding mechanism for the wingtip had, for some reason, been left in place!

The Model 32 retained the A6M2's armament of two 7.7mm Type 97 machine guns and two 20mm Type 99-1 cannon, but increased the weapon's supply of ammunition to a drum containing 100 rounds per gun in response to requests from operational units.

To Mitsubishi's disappointment, the A6M3, although having improved lateral control at higher speeds, proved to be only marginally faster than the A6M2. This was primarily due to the weight of the larger Sakae 21 engine and the increased ammunition load. The reduction in size of the fuselage fuel tank to accommodate the Sakae 21, and the engine's increased fuel consumption compared to the Sakae 12, resulted in a drop in the Zero-sen's range from 1,930 miles in the A6M2 Model 21 to 1,477 miles in the A6M3 Model 32. This proved to be disastrous for units flying A6M3 Model 32s from Buin in the Guadalcanal campaign.

A6M3 MODEL 22

The A6M3 Model 22 was a hurried response to urgent requests from the field to restore the Zero-sen's range so as to enable the new model to reach Guadalcanal from Japanese bases in Rabaul. Mitsubishi restored the long wing of the A6M2, placing a small 12-gallon fuel tank in each wingtip. This gave the new Model 22, so designated because of its return to the earlier type of rounded wing, the longest range of any of the Zero-sen models. The first A6M3 Model 22s left the Mitsubishi factory at the end of 1942. The majority of the 560 examples that Mitsubishi built retained the same armament as the Model 32, but some of the later production airplanes switched to the more powerful Type 99-2 20mm cannon.

A6M5 MODEL 52

Built in greater numbers than any other model of Zero-sen, the A6M5 Model 52 was an attempt to upgrade the aircraft's performance in the face of increasing numbers of

Intended as a fast-climbing interceptor fighter, the Mitsubishi J2M3 Interceptor Fighter Raiden (Thunderbolt) Model 21 was superior to the A6M5 both in terms of performance and armament, but it suffered from protracted development delays and was built in only small numbers. (Peter M. Bowers Collection, Museum of Flight)

second-generation American fighters, while simplifying production. The Model 52 retained the basic fuselage structure of the earlier models, but featured a shorter-span, redesigned wing with rounded wingtips. The folding wing mechanism was removed completely and the ailerons faired into the outboard wingtip. Mitsubishi increased the thickness of the wing skinning to allow an increase in the diving speed to 410mph.

Four fuel tanks in the wings, the main tank next to the fuselage and a smaller tank outboard helped retain the Zero-sen's long range with the shorter wing. After the 371st production aircraft, Mitsubishi installed a CO_2 fire-extinguishing system to protect the fuel tanks in the wings, with CO_2 tanks located behind the cockpit.

The Model 52 used the Nakajima Sakae 21 engine, but with individual exhaust stacks, producing a higher maximum speed of 351mph. Armament remained the same as in late Model 22 aircraft, consisting of two 7.7mm Type 97 machine guns in the nose and two Type 99-2 20mm cannon in the wings, firing a more powerful projectile with increased muzzle velocity. The A6M5 Model 52 was put into production by Mitsubishi in August 1943, while Nakajima began producing Model 52s from February 1944.

A6M5 MODEL 52a

Roman letters a, b and c were used to identify subsequent models of the A6M5. The Model 52 entered combat just as the US Navy was introducing the F6F-3 Hellcat, resulting in IJNAF units soon calling for even better performance from the Zero-sen. There was little the already over-stretched Mitsubishi design team could do in the way of introducing substantive improvements, however, and the IJNAF, desperate for more fighters, was reluctant to disrupt production. The Model 52a was a stopgap, with only minor modifications. The thickness of the wing skinning was increased to allow an even higher diving speed, while the ammunition feed for the two Type 99-2 20mm

This underside view of an A6M5 Model 52 reveals the staple IJNAF fighter in near-perfect planform. The Model 52 was the most prolific of all Zero-sen variants, with more than 6,000 examples being built. (via Aerospace Publishing)

wing cannon was switched from a 100-round drum to a belt-fed system containing 125 rounds per weapon. The latter was redesignated the Type 99-2 Model 4 cannon. The first production aircraft left the factory in March 1944.

A6M5 MODEL 52b

The Model 52b was another hurried attempt to improve the Zero-sen without major modifications. For the first time, the IJNAF approved a change in armament. In developing the Zero-sen, the IJNAF had jumped from the 7.7mm machine gun directly to the 20mm cannon, skipping the intermediate heavier machine gun class in favor of the more powerful cannon intended for destroying heavier bombers. In high-speed fighter-versus-fighter combat against the Hellcat and the Corsair, the slower-firing 20mm cannon was not as effective.

In the Model 52b, the IJNAF removed one of the nose-mounted 7.7mm Type 97 machine guns and replaced it with a single 13.2 mm Type 3 machine gun – a development of the Browning 0.50in. machine gun with a rate of fire of 800 rounds a minute, compared to 490 rounds a minute for the 20mm Type 99-2 cannon. For protection against frontal attacks, Mitsubishi added a two-inch thick armored windscreen built from two layers of plastic sandwiched between two sheets of glass.

The A6M5 Model 52b went into production in April 1944, the IJNAF hoping that the newer version of the Zero-sen would improve its fortunes in its next battle with the US Navy. This turned out to be the disastrous Battle of the Philippine Sea in June 1944.

A6M5 MODEL 52c

The Model 52c was the result of the IJNAF's urgent need for further upgrades of the Zero-sen due to delays in finding a replacement fighter. The IJNAF insisted on improvements in armament, armor protection, an additional fuel tank and increased diving speeds, but refused Mitsubishi's request for a more powerful engine to counter the increase in weight from these changes.

The A6M5 Model 52c was another effort to squeeze more performance out of the Zero-sen, with a thicker wing skinning allowing an increase in diving speed and improved armament of one nose-mounted 13.2mm Type 3 machine gun and a single Type 3 in each wing outboard of the 20mm Type 99-2 cannon. (Peter M. Bowers Collection, Museum of Flight)

31

For the Model 52c, Mitsubishi installed two 13.2mm Type 3 machine guns in the wings outboard of the 20mm cannon, with 240 rounds per gun. The remaining 7.7mm machine gun in the nose was removed to save weight. Finally addressing the problem of protection for the Zero-sen's pilot, Mitsubishi installed a sheet of armor plate behind the pilot's seat and fitted armored glass panels behind the headrest. The system of fuel tanks was rearranged to keep the Zero-sen's center of gravity within acceptable limits, a 31-gallon tank being added in mid-fuselage and the capacity of the wing fuel tanks reduced. Attachment points for air-to-air rockets were fitted under the wings. All these changes added more than 600lb to the gross weight of the Model 52c.

The IJNAF hoped to install the Nakajima Sakae 31 engine in the Model 52c, which would have generated 1,210hp with water-menthol injection, but this powerplant failed its tests and could not be made ready in time. Production of the Model 52c began in September 1944. Unsurprisingly, performance of the Model 52c deteriorated due to the added weight, and pilots complained that the Zero-sen had lost some of its superlative handling qualities.

A6M5 ZERO-SEN MODEL 52 COWLING/WING GUNS

The A6M5 Model 52 retained the basic armament of the earlier models of the Zero-sen, with two 7.7mm Type 97 machine guns in the nose. Ammunition boxes held 700 rounds per gun. The two Type 99-2 20mm cannon in the wings featured a longer barrel than the earlier Type 99-1, with approximately 18in. of the weapon extending out of the wing leading edge. The Model 52's cannon were drum-fed, with a drum containing 100 rounds for each weapon.

A6M7 MODEL 63

The Model 63 Zero-sen was a hurriedly developed replacement for the obsolescent Aichi D3A Type 99 Carrier Bomber ("Val"), the A6M7 having a slower landing speed than the faster Yokosuka D4Y Carrier Bomber ("Judy"), which in turn meant that it could operate from smaller aircraft carriers. The IJNAF had hastily modified the Zero-sen to carry a 250kg bomb in place of the centerline drop tank, and it used the Model 63 in the Philippines from late 1944 despite the modification encountering numerous problems. Mitsubishi subsequently designed a more effective bomb-release mechanism, strengthened the horizontal tail and replaced the centerline drop tank with two tanks under the wings.

F6F-3 and A6M5 Type 0 Carrier Fighter Model 52 Comparison Specifications

	F6F-3 Hellcat	A6M5 Type 0 Model 52
Powerplant	2,000hp Pratt & Whitney R-2800-10	1,130hp Nakajima Sakae 21
Dimensions		
Span	42ft 10in.	36ft 1in.
Length	33ft 7in.	29ft 11in.
Height	13ft 1in.	11ft 6in.
Wing Area	334 sq. ft	229 sq. ft
Weights		
Empty	8,951lb	4,136lb
Loaded	12,213lb	6,025lb
Performance		
Max Speed	375mph at 23,700ft	351mph at 19,685ft
Range	1,620 miles with drop tank	1,194 miles
Climb	to 25,000ft in 14 minutes	to 19,685ft in 7 minutes
Service Ceiling	37,500ft	38,520ft
Armament	6 x 0.50in. Browning M-2 machine guns	2 x 7.7mm Type 99 machine guns and 2 x 20mm Type 99-2 cannon

THE STRATEGIC SITUATION

A US Marine Corps F4F-4 Wildcat taxis past USAAF P-38 Lightnings on Guadalcanal in 1943. With the arrival of the P-38 and, especially, the Vought F4U Corsair in the South Pacific the Allies had fighters with performance superior to the Zero-sen. Their appearance in combat occurred just as Allied forces began shifting to the offensive. (127 GR-3-52842, RG 127, NARA)

By the end of 1942, the pre-war fleets with which the IJNAF and the US Navy had gone to war on December 7, 1941 had fought themselves to the point of exhaustion. The US Navy had lost four fleet carriers (USS *Lexington* (CV-2), USS *Yorktown* (CV-5), USS *Wasp* (CV-7) and USS *Hornet* (CV-8)), leaving only USS *Saratoga* (CV-3)

and USS *Enterprise* (CV-6) in the Pacific. The IJNAF had lost *Shoho, Akagi, Kaga, Hiryu, Soryu* and *Ryujo*.

American forces had invaded Guadalcanal in August 1942 in a limited offensive, and subsequently held the island against repeated Japanese attempts to defeat them until the latter decided to abandon it in early 1943. To the west of the Solomon Islands, American and Australian forces had held New Guinea and prevented the Japanese from capturing the main base at Port Moresby. In aerial battles over New Guinea and Guadalcanal, the aviation units of the IJNAF had failed to gain air superiority and had suffered a steady attrition of experienced pilots Japan could ill afford to lose.

For the first six months of 1943 there would be no significant movement in the relative positions of the Japanese and Allied forces in the Pacific. However, the Japanese were slowly but steadily pushed onto the defensive, losing their foothold in the Aleutians, their forces in eastern New Guinea weakening and IJNAF fighter units failing to re-assert air superiority over the Allied air forces through Operation *I-Go* in April 1943.

Japan's strategy in World War II, once its army and navy had captured the vital resources of Southeast Asia, was to establish a defensive barrier stretching from the Aleutian Islands south through the Central Pacific and west through the Solomon and Bismarck Islands and New Guinea to the Netherlands East Indies, then up through Malaya and Burma to the border with India. Japan intended to fight a defensive war, defeating the inevitable American response as it moved across the Pacific and wearing down American forces through attrition to exhaustion, at which point the US government

Adm Isoroku Yamamoto, Commander-in-Chief of the IJN's Combined Fleet, salutes Japanese pilots on Rabaul on April 18, 1943. His visit to Rabaul coincided with Operation *I-Go*, an attempt to regain air superiority over the Solomons that failed. Yamamoto was killed later that same day when P-38 Lightnings shot down his airplane. (via the author)

The Pacific battleground. In a little less than two years the US Navy's Fast Carrier Task Force swept across the Pacific Ocean, supporting the capture of key island bases along the way, blasting the sea and air forces of the IJN in a relentless battle of attrition and, after the capture of the Philippines and Okinawa, attacking the Japanese home islands as a prelude to invasion.

would have to negotiate a peace favorable to Japan. The IJN intended to use its submarine force and long-range aircraft flying from its island bases in the Central Pacific to weaken the American naval force as it headed west, thus allowing the battleships and carriers of the IJN's Combined Fleet to destroy the US Navy's Pacific Fleet in a decisive battle.

American strategy in the war against Japan was based on War Plan Orange, the pre-war document the US military had developed over several decades that outlined a plan for the defeat of Japan, codenamed "Orange". The central tenet of the plan was that America would wage a maritime war against Japan. With remarkable prescience, the plan outlined the three phases the course of a probable war with Japan would take.

In Phase I, Japan would seize American possessions in the Pacific, including the Philippines, and critical sources of raw materials in Southeast Asia. In Phase II, a powerful American naval and air force would march across the Central Pacific, capturing islands in the Gilberts, Marshalls, and Carolines to establish bases for the fleet and secure supply lines, ultimately recapturing positions in the Philippines to establish a blockade to cut Japan off from its sources of raw materials. Finally, in Phase III, the

American force would capture islands closer to Japan to tighten the blockade and to serve as bases for an aerial campaign aimed at the destruction of Japan's industry.

A key difference in perspective of the competing Japanese and American strategies was the timeframe. While Japan planned, and hoped, for a short and victorious war, the American plans envisioned a campaign across the Central Pacific that would take two to three years, if not longer, and that would require the full resources of the nation.

In the event, Japanese actions and success during the first year following the attack on Pearl Harbor turned out to be similar to what was expected in Phase I of the earlier War Plan Orange. Japanese forces overwhelmed the weaker US Army Air Corps and US Navy forces in the Pacific, with the loss of American island bases and the Philippines. Japan succeeded in establishing a defensive barrier that America could not penetrate with the forces initially available in the early months of the conflict.

Japan's attack had caught America preparing, but unprepared, for war. In order to execute the planned strategy for war against Japan, American forces had to fight defensively until such time as sufficient arms had been built and men trained to launch Phase II of the plan – the attack across the Central Pacific. To add to America's challenge, the original Plan Orange had not envisioned any fighting in the Southwest Pacific, but the need to ensure the line of communications between the United States and Australia, and the defense of Australia itself, brought American troops, airplanes and ships to New Guinea and the Solomon Islands.

An F6F-3 from VF-5 prepares to land back aboard *Yorktown* in the late summer of 1943. This vessel was one of the new *Essex* class fleet carriers that arrived at Pearl Harbor at that time. VF-5 would be one of the first carrier-based Hellcat squadrons to take the new Grumman fighter into combat. (Robert Lawson Collection, National Naval Aviation Museum)

A6M2 Model 21 and A6M3 Model 22 Zero-sens at Kahili airfield on the island of Bougainville in 1943. The IJNAF was now committed to a relentless battle of attrition it could ill afford. In the air combats over the Solomon Islands and Rabaul the IJNAF lost far too many of its most experienced pilots and leaders. (via the author)

Fortunately, before the attack on Pearl Harbor the US Navy had begun to lay the foundation for what would become the most powerful fleet the world had ever seen. In February 1940, it had placed an order for USS *Essex* (CV-9), the first of a new class of large fleet aircraft carriers developed from the earlier *Yorktown* class. The US Navy ordered three more carriers in this class (CV-10, -11 and -12) in May 1940, and after the passage of the Two Ocean Navy Act (which approved an increase in the US Navy's authorized air strength to 15,000 aircraft in June–July 1940) it ordered seven more (CVs -13 to -19). Two more *Essex* class carriers were ordered in the weeks following the Pearl Harbor attack, with an additional ten ordered in August 1942.

To equip the air groups that would form the striking power of the new carriers, the US Navy contracted with Grumman for a new torpedo-bomber (the TBF Avenger), with Curtiss for a new dive-bomber (the SB2C Helldiver), Chance Vought for a new carrier fighter (the F4U Corsair) and, in 1941, placed another order with Grumman for the XF6F-1.

It took time for this new aircraft carrier fleet, and accompanying subsidiary vessels, to be built and commissioned into service with fully trained crews. Originally, *Essex* was due to be completed in March 1944, but with the declaration of war with Japan and the conversion of the American economy to a war footing, the vessel was commissioned at the end of December 1942. Other aircraft carriers in the same class followed during 1943–44. As a wartime expedient, the US Navy ordered the conversion of light cruiser hulls then under construction into a new class of light carriers. The first carrier in this class, USS *Independence* (CV-22), was commissioned in January 1943. By August, the US Navy had commissioned six more light carriers.

The larger *Essex* class fleet carriers had air groups composed of three squadrons – a fighter squadron (VF) with 36 F6F Hellcats, a dive-bomber squadron (VB) with 36 SBD Dauntlesses or SB2C Helldivers, and a torpedo-bomber squadron (VT) with 18 TBM Avengers. The light carriers had a smaller air group with 24 Hellcats and nine TBM Avengers.

The IJN, too, was attempting to re-arm, but thanks to the disparity in industrial capacity the US Navy pulled ahead, rapidly and in quantity. It is interesting to note that in the opening stages of the Battle for Okinawa in April 1945, only one of the eleven fleet carriers and six light carriers in Task Force 58 (the US Navy's Fast Carrier Task Force) had been completed prior to the attack on Pearl Harbor.

The US Navy's new carriers – *Essex*, USS *Yorktown* (CV-10), *Lexington* (CV-16) and the light carriers *Independence*, USS *Princeton* (CVL-23) and USS *Belleau Wood* (CVL-24) – began arriving at Pearl Harbor during the summer of 1943.

Along with the build-up of this powerful new force came questions about its deployment and doctrine. In the pre-war doctrine, the US Navy's aircraft carriers had been subordinated to the battleship fleet that most traditional US Navy officers thought would play the decisive role in any naval action against the Japanese fleet. Partly because of the scarcity of carriers, and fears about their vulnerability to land-based aircraft, aircraft carriers operated in single carrier task groups. The loss of battleships at Pearl Harbor and the battles of the Coral Sea and Midway put paid to pre-war thinking. The naval war against Japan would be a carrier war. The air officers under Adm Chester Nimitz, Commander-in-Chief Pacific Fleet, now argued for multi-carrier task groups and an independent, offensive role for the carriers as the fleet's main weapon. The objectives of the carrier force were to attack Japanese land bases and surface fleets and to establish air superiority in support of amphibious operations.

The Joint Chiefs of Staff had decided on a strategy for deployment of the carrier force. There would be two parallel advances across the Pacific – Gen Douglas MacArthur and Adm William Halsey would conduct an offensive in the Southwest Pacific to neutralize the Japanese positions in the Solomon and Bismarck islands and New Guinea, while Adm Nimitz would advance across the Central Pacific, capturing island bases in the Gilberts and the Marshalls, and Truk, in the Carolines. The ultimate objective of both advances was to establish a position – either in the Philippines, on Formosa or along the China coast – to cut the flow of supplies to Japan. Before these objectives could be achieved there were still many issues to be resolved concerning carrier doctrine, combat tactics and logistics, not least of which was the question of whether the new F6F Hellcat could wrest air superiority from the A6M Zero-sen in the coming aerial battles.

THE COMBATANTS

US NAVY PILOT TRAINING

Following the attack on Pearl Harbor, Secretary of the Navy Franklin Knox approved an expanded training program to produce 20,000 Naval Aviators annually. Rather than train a small cadre of pilots to an exceptional standard, the US Navy chose to train a much larger group of men to a high standard to ensure an adequate and timely flow of replacement pilots to the fleet. America had the resources in men and airplanes to make possible a vast expansion in the number of Naval Aviators reaching fleet units.

The US Navy had already begun to simplify its training syllabus before the Pearl Harbor attack in an effort to speed up training. It initially reduced the instruction period from one year to seven months by shifting Primary and Basic training to landplanes rather than floatplanes and making cadets specialize in a particular type of aircraft during advanced training. In February 1942 the Bureau of Aeronautics adopted an aviation training program that lasted eleven-and-a-half months, with trainees destined for single-engined airplanes spending three months in pre-flight training, three months in Primary, three-and-a-half months in Intermediate and two to three months in Operational training after attending pre-flight school and elementary flight training.

By the end of 1942 the US Navy had four functional training commands – Air Primary Training, Air Intermediate Training, Air Operational Training and Air Technical Training. At the end of 1943 these all became part of the Naval Air Training Command.

Most prospective pilot trainees entered the US Navy through the pre-war V-5 Naval Reserve program. In January 1942 the US Navy established four pre-flight

After completing their Primary and Basic Intermediate training phases, US Navy aviation cadets selected for carriers moved on to fly the Curtiss SNC and the North American SNJ in Advanced Intermediate training. (80G-472821, RG80, NARA)

schools around the country to conduct classes in the principles of flight, internal combustion engines, aerodynamics, aerology, communications and navigation, as well as intensive physical conditioning. In the fall of 1942, with a rapidly increasing number of trainees, the US Navy introduced two early training programs that aviation cadets would complete before going to pre-flight school. The Flight Preparatory School program provided 15 weeks of introductory classes in the topics to be covered in pre-flight school, as well as physical conditioning. After completing this course, the aviation cadet received 12 weeks of elementary flight training in J-3 Piper Cubs, covering 22 hours of duel instruction and 14 hours of solo time, through the Civilian Pilot Training program, which had been renamed the War Training Service.

Formal pre-flight school consisted of 11 weeks of ground school covering the same topics introduced at the Naval Flight Preparatory Schools, but at a more advanced level, combined with continued physical conditioning. From pre-flight school, the aviation cadet entered primary flight training, where he received some 80 hours of instruction on primary training airplanes, principally the Naval Aircraft Factory N3N (the famous "Yellow Peril") or the Stearman N2S. The goal of the primary training phase was to teach the aviation cadet how to fly safely, smoothly and with precision in all maneuvers. In the final stages of primary instruction the cadet practiced formation and night flying.

In Intermediate flight training the goal was to turn the aviation cadet into a military pilot. The four weeks in the Basic phase of Intermediate training were spent mastering the Vultee SNV Valiant, a monoplane trainer that bridged the gap between the biplanes in primary and more powerful aircraft that lay ahead. At this stage the aviation cadet practiced more advanced formation and divisional tactics,

41

completing ten hours of duel instruction and 22 hours solo, and then began instrument flying training in the Link trainer. In the Advanced phase of Intermediate flight training, cadets selected for carrier aircraft moved on to the Curtiss SNC and the North American SNJ Texan, where they were introduced to simulated carrier landings, aerial gunnery, advanced navigation and basic combat tactics. On completion of the Intermediate training stage, involving 14 hours of duel and 86 hours of solo flying, the cadet was awarded his Wings of Gold and received a commission as an ensign in the US Navy or as a second lieutenant in the US Marine Corps.

Naval Aviators selected for fighter training went to one of a number of airfields in Florida for their Operational training, which consisted of around 100 hours in service-type airplanes. As the fleet had first call on the latest production fighters, until production exceeded fleet demand the Operational training command had to use older fighter types like the Brewster F2A Buffalo and the earlier models of the F4F Wildcat.

Aviation cadets began practicing aerial gunnery in Advanced Intermediate training in order to learn standard gunnery approaches. Flying SNJs armed with a 0.30in. machine gun, cadets fired color-coded rounds at the target sleeve – they are shown here counting up their hits. (80G-475244, RG80, NARA)

Operational training consisted of three phases – mastery of the service-type airplane, intensive instruction in combat skills including gunnery, navigation, night flying and carrier landings, and training in combat tactics. Ground school covered training in tactics, gunnery, aircraft recognition and related topics. Carrier qualification required eight successful takeoffs and landings. One of the great benefits of the operational training phase was the US Navy's practice of assigning returned combat pilots as instructors to pass on their experience. After completion of Operational training, and with a total of around 350 flying hours, the Naval Aviator would normally be assigned to a fighter squadron in a carrier air group working up for deployment with the fleet. Here, the new pilot would receive more intensive training in fighter tactics and gunnery before entering combat.

During the war the US Navy put great emphasis on aerial gunnery, and particularly deflection shooting. In the Advanced phase of Intermediate training, the aviation cadet began practicing basic gunnery approaches with an instructor, moving on to firing live ammunition at tow-target sleeves with color-coded 0.30in. bullets.

Concerned with the availability of service fighter aircraft for training, the US Navy turned to synthetic training devices, the forerunners of flight simulators. One of these, the Gunairstructor, was developed for aerial gunnery training. The student sat in a mock-up of a fighter cockpit with a stick, throttle, rudder pedals and a gunsight, with a view forward to a screen showing a section of sea and sky. An instructor sat just forward of the cockpit mock-up with similar controls. A projector threw a silhouette of an enemy airplane onto the screen that the instructor could manipulate to make it fly in any direction. The student pilot could practice deflection shooting by "flying" his airplane to keep the enemy airplane in his gunsight. The instructor could demonstrate the correct aiming point for different deflection angles. Although

43

1. Upper left cockpit light
2. Rudder trim tab control
3. Cowl flaps control
4. Oil cooler/intercooler shutters control
5. Droppable fuel tank release switch
6. Mask microphone switch
7. Throttle control
8. Mixture control
9. Wing flap electrical switch
10. Supercharger control
11. Water injection control switch
12. Elevator trim tab control
13. Aileron trim tab control
14. Fuel tank pressurizing control
15. Propeller pitch control
16. Fuel selector valve dial
17. Reserve fuel tank pressurizing control
18. Fuel tank selector valve control
19. Oil dilution switch
20. Propeller pitch vernier control
21. Engine control quadrant friction knob
22. Auxiliary electric fuel pump switch
23. Cabin sliding hood control
24. Battery switch
25. Main electrical distribution panel
26. Electrical light panel
27. Radio controls
28. Recognition lights
29. Hand pump selector valve
30. Aft right cockpit shelf light
31. Manual reset circuit breaker panel
32. Access to reverse current relay
33. Hydraulic hand pump
34. Armament panel
35. Hand microphone
36. Pyrotechnic cartridge clips
37. Radio controls
38. IFF destruction switch
39. Carburetor protracted air control
40. Ignition switch
41. Clock
42. Landing gear emergency control
43. Directional gyro
44. Compass
45. Mk 8 electric gunsight
46. Attitude gyro
47. Chart board light
48. Attitude gyro caging knob
49. Tachometer
50. Water quantity gauge (A.D.I. System)
51. Instrument panel fluorescent lights
52. Cylinder head temperature gauge
53. Oil pressure gauge
54. Landing gear and wing flap position indicator
55. Landing gear control
56. Altimeter
57. Rudder pedals
58. Airspeed indicator
59. Gun charging controls
60. Cockpit heater control
61. Turn and bank indicator
62. Ammunition rounds counter
63. Fluorescent lights control
64. Rate of climb indicator
65. Wing lock safety control handle
66. Manifold pressure gauge
67. Chart board (retracted)
68. Oil temperature gauge
69. Fuel pressure gauge
70. Fuel quantity gauge
71. Control column

A6M5 ZERO-SEN COCKPIT

1. Type 98 reflector gunsight
2. Artificial horizon
3. Turn and bank indicator
4. Type 99 7.7mm machine guns
5. High-altitude automatic mixture control
6. Exhaust temperature gauge
7. Clock
8. Airspeed indicator
9. Magnetic compass
10. Rate of climb indicator
11. Fuel and oil pressure gauge
12. Tachometer

13. Emergency fuel pump lever
14. Direction finder control unit
15. Emergency power boost
16. Radio direction indicator
17. Magneto switch
18. Altimeter
19. Control column
20. Manifold pressure gauge
21. Oil temperature gauge
22. Cylinder head temperature gauge
23. Cockpit lights
24. Throttle quadrant/20mm cannon firing lever

25. Primer
26. Oxygen supply gauge
27. Hydraulic pressure gauge
28. Oxygen control
29. Oil cooler shutter control
30. Cowl flap control
31. Radio control unit
32. Elevator trimming tab control
33. Circuit breakers
34. Rudder pedals
35. Wing tanks cooling air intake control
36. Emergency gear down lever
37. Loop antenna handle

38. Seat up/down lever
39. Fuel tank jettison handle
40. Fuselage tank fuel gauge
41. Wing tanks fuel gauge
42. Emergency fuel jettison lever
43. Fuselage/wing tanks switching cock
44. Wing tanks selector valve
45. Bomb release levers
46. Seat
47. Arresting hook winding wheel
48. Wing tank fuel switching cock
49. 20mm cannon master switch

simplistic and likened to an arcade game, it proved effective, as one Hellcat pilot flying with VF-31 over Kwajalein explained in the following report:

> On my first combat action over Roi airfield, on Kwajalein, I made a stern run on a "Zeke" from the "seven o'clock" position. As I neared firing range I immediately recognized the shot as one I had seen many times in the Gunairstructor, in which the point of aim is just over the port wingtip. Accordingly, I put the pipper of my gunsight over the "Zeke's" port wingtip and pressed the trigger. The results looked like a gunnery training film. My tracers streamed out in a neat curve to the right and hits from the incendiary bullets flashed along the "Zeke's" engine cowling and fuselage. He started down smoking and my wingman jumped in and blew him up.
>
> The Gunairstructor practice enabled me to recognize this shot instantly and shoot immediately without any preliminary mental calculations about the correct mil lead for this particular deflection problem, which is frequently under-led as a no-deflection shot.

IJNAF PILOT TRAINING

The IJN's strategy for a war with America was based on the assumption that the conflict would be short and decisive. Japanese forces would inflict a series of rapid and punishing defeats that would force the United States to negotiate peace terms favorable to Japan. The IJNAF had long emphasized quality over quantity for its air units, preferring to build a small force of exceptional pilots equipped with superior weapons like the Zero-sen. This view conformed to the theory of the short war, decisive victory basis of Japanese strategy, and also reflected the realities of Japan's industrial capacity. It could never hope to match American industrial might, and in a war of attrition Japan would inevitably lose. In the years leading up to Japan's

The majority of the IJNAF's pilots were enlisted men. This group of trainee pilots stands next to a Yokosuka K5Y1 Type 93 Intermediate Trainer. (Author's collection)

decision to go to war with America, there were few in the IJN's high command who accepted that a long war would be the likely outcome.

At the outbreak of the war, the IJNAF's training system was turning out around 2,000 pilots a year. For enlisted trainees – the bulk of its pilot force – the training program at this time began with one to two years of pre-flight training for new enlistees, six months for enlisted men and two to four months for officers. Primary and Basic training lasted for six months, enlisted trainees receiving 44 hours of flying in the Yokosuka K2Y2 Primary Trainer and the Yokosuka K5Y1/2 Type 93 Intermediate Trainer, while officer trainees received 60 hours at this stage. Some sources state that after the war began the goal for Primary and Basic training was to give trainees a total of 100 flying hours. The Operational training phase lasted another four to six months, with trainees getting around 100 hours flying older service types.

Having been assigned to a specialized airplane type, new pilots received a further 150 hours of tactical flight training in operational units – often new units in the process of formation – where they would continue to perfect their combat skills.

During the war the IJNAF had only limited numbers of Kyushu K10W1 advanced trainers (a licensed-built, locally revised North American NA-16, equivalent to the US Navy's SNJ Texan). Instead, the IJNAF favored using two-seat versions of its fighters to train neophyte fighter pilots. In the first two years of the war, new fighter pilots began training on the Mitsubishi A5M4-K, a two-seat version of the Type 96 fighter, before moving on to the single-seat version to develop their skills. During 1943, the IJNAF contracted with the Dai-Jijuichi K.K. to build a

No fewer than 5,770 examples of the Type 93 Intermediate Trainer were built between 1933 and 1945. Later in the war 176 Kyushu K10W1s (licensed-built North American NA-16 monoplane trainers modified specifically for IJNAF use) supplemented the Type 93s. (Author's collection)

two-seat version of the Zero-sen as the A6M2-K. Beginning in November 1943, Dai-Jijuichi built 236 A6M2-Ks, with the Hitachi Kokuki K.K. building a further 272. Retaining only the nose-mounted Type 97 7.7mm machine guns, the A6M2-K had a maximum speed of 296mph.

The IJNAF went to war with around 3,000 trained pilots, with the best allocated to its carrier air groups, but without an adequate reserve. Before the attack on Pearl Harbor, the IJNAF had intended to vastly expand its training system to produce 15,000 pilots a year, but this plan fell by the wayside as Japanese forces advanced across the Pacific and Southeast Asia.

Remarkably, once at war the IJNAF did little to expand pilot training, adding only two new training groups in late 1942 and early 1943. The training system produced around 2,300 pilots during 1942 and 2,700 during 1943. In contrast, the US Navy added more than 5,000 pilots in 1942 and nearly 12,000 in 1943. The IJNAF's training system could not keep pace with the attrition in the battles over the Solomon Islands, and with the loss of so many experienced aviators, the quality of the pilots began an inexorable decline. As losses mounted, pilots were rushed from training units to the frontline after completing only limited tuition, particularly in aerial gunnery.

Unlike the US Navy, the IJNAF had no policy of rotating pilots or units in and out of combat after a certain period or number of missions. Units remained in combat until they were decimated, pilots flying until they were wounded or killed, or succumbed to physical exhaustion.

(Source – United States Strategic Bombing Survey (Pacific): *Japanese Air Power*)

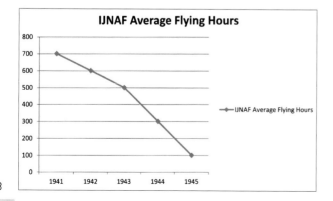

A small number returned to Japan to serve as instructors or to join new units. The loss of experienced pilots and inadequate training only increased the rate of attrition, creating what historian Mark Peattie has called "a downward-spiraling vicious cycle". There were too few combat-experienced instructors available to pass on the lessons they had learned to new trainees. When these younger pilots entered combat lacking the skills they needed, there were too few experienced leaders to help them survive, leading to even more rapid attrition.

Belatedly, the IJNAF started expanding its training program in late 1943 and early 1944, drawing on conscription of high school and university students. The IJNAF increased the number of training groups from 15 to 48, as well as the number of airplanes allocated to the training groups, but there were never enough training airplanes and qualified instructors. As the war rolled into its third year, there were increasing shortages of fuel, cutting flying hours for both training air groups and tactical units. The result was a continuous decline in pilot quality.

By 1944, when newly minted US Navy Hellcat pilots were entering combat with 500 or more flying hours, their IJNAF counterparts were joining their units with 300 flying hours or less. The Zero-sen was a relatively straightforward and forgiving aircraft to fly, but getting the best out of it, particularly against a superior fighter like the Hellcat, required considerable training. As the war went on, fewer and fewer Zero-sen pilots acquired the necessary level of skill to do this.

The IJNAF made extensive use of two-seat fighters to bridge the gap between the Type 93 trainer and operational airplanes. The A6M2-K provided an introduction to flying the Zero-sen. (Jack Lambert Collection, Museum of Flight)

COMBAT

US NAVY FIGHTER TACTICS

By the time the Hellcat went into combat in the fall of 1943, the US Navy had nearly a year's worth of experience of combat with the Zero-sen, and from this experience it had drawn up standard defensive and offensive tactics against fighters for a single plane, a section or a division. These tactics were further distilled into a few fundamental principles that could be easily understood, practiced repeatedly and employed in combat.

Defensively, the single pilot's goal was to foil the enemy's attack and ideally to maneuver into a position to launch a counterattack. The first fundamental principle taught to neophyte fighter pilots was the importance of having a definite, well-thought-out plan of action, based on an understanding of the relative performance of the enemy fighter and one's own. Knowing the relative performance advantages and disadvantages of an enemy airplane was vital to determining what defensive action to take in relation to the anticipated movements of the enemy. As the US Navy's training booklet put it,

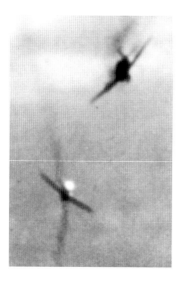

This gun camera footage shows a Hellcat diving down to attack a Zero-sen. US Navy tactics stressed attacking with an altitude advantage, using two fighters or two sections to bracket the enemy. (80G-46981, RG80, NARA)

"There is no percentage in dogfighting an opponent who can outmaneuver you". Pilots were rigorously drilled in how to anticipate the movements of an enemy fighter, and how to respond accordingly. In the US Navy's words, "you haven't any time to work out tactical problems by higher mathematics when you have a Zero on your tail".

The second fundamental principle was that all defensive actions should begin with a turn into the enemy's attack in order to present a more difficult deflection shot. If jumped from behind, US Navy and US Marine Corps Wildcat pilots had learned that a high-speed diving turn to the right could shake off a Zero-sen, as at increased speeds the ailerons of the IJNAF fighter stiffened markedly. An even more effective defensive move was to initiate a turn to the left, and once the Zero-sen pilot was committed, immediately turn to the right. Hellcat pilots adopted the same tactics to escape a Zero-sen on their tail.

The US Navy's basic fighting unit was the section of two airplanes, and the essence of section tactics was teamwork. While a pilot might find himself on his own in combat, and therefore had to know how to react defensively, the training stressed over and over again that pilots should not seek to fly or fight on their own but always as a member of a team. Defensive tactics for a section were based on the beam defense that Lt Cdr John Thach had developed and proven at the Battle of Midway, and that was more commonly known as the "Thach Weave". Hellcat squadrons arriving on the

DAVID McCAMPBELL

Cdr David McCampbell was the US Navy's leading ace of World War II, and the highest scoring Hellcat pilot against the Zero-sen.

Born in 1910 in Bessemer, Alabama, McCampbell graduated from the US Naval Academy in 1933 and then served for four years on a cruiser before becoming a Naval Aviator, receiving his wings in 1938. His first assignment was to VF-4, flying Grumman fighters aboard USS *Ranger* (CV-4). In 1940 McCampbell transferred to the air group on board USS *Wasp* (CV-7), taking on the role of Landing Signals Officer and surviving the sinking of the vessel in September 1942. Promoted to lieutenant commander in October 1942, McCampbell served as an instructor in the US Navy's Operational Training Command, teaching would-be fighter pilots.

In September 1943 McCampbell commissioned VF-15 and became its first CO. Promoted to commander in January 1944, he took over Carrier Air Group (CVG) 15 in February and led it during a six-month combat tour on board USS *Essex* (CV-9) from April to November 1944.

A highly experienced pilot before he entered combat, McCampbell claimed his first aerial victory – a Zero-sen – over Saipan on June 11, 1944. Eight days later, during the Great Marianas Turkey Shoot, McCampbell shot down five D4Y1 "Judy" dive-bombers in the morning and claimed two "Zekes" shot down over Guam in the afternoon. On June 23 he shot down a "Zeke" and shared in the destruction of a second A6M west of Guam. During the first carrier strikes against the Philippines he shot down two "Zekes", a "Jack" and a Ki-46 "Dinah".

McCampbell's most famous combat took place on October 24, 1944 when a formation of more than 60 IJNAF fighters, dive-bombers and torpedo-bombers launched an attack against Task Force 58. Following the formation as it headed back to Manila, McCampbell and his wingman, Lt(jg) Roy Rushing, maintained a position above the weaving Japanese fighters and proceeded to make repeated passes against any who "1) attempted to climb up to our altitude, 2) scissored outside the support of others, 3) straggled and 4) became too eager and came up at us singly". After an hour McCampbell had shot down nine fighters and Rushing six – a feat that won McCampbell the Medal of Honor. He had claimed five "Zekes", two "Hamps" and two "Oscars" in the fight. He claimed his last "Zeke" on November 5, 1944,

bringing his total claims against the Zero-sen to 14.5 (there is a strong possibility that the fighters McCampbell and Rushing encountered on October 24 were in fact all A6M5 Zero-sens, which would raise McCampbell's total to 16.5).

McCampbell remained in the US Navy after the war, retiring as a captain in 1964. He passed away on June 30, 1996.

(80G-258197, RG80, NARA)

YOSHINAO KODAIRA

Yoshinao Kodaira was born in Nagano Prefecture, to the west of Tokyo, in 1918. In 1935 he enlisted in the IJN, joining its paymaster corps, where he served for several years before entering flight training. Kodaira was a member of the 43rd Pilot Training course, graduating in November 1938 and moving on to Operational training as a fighter pilot with the Saeki and Oita Kokutai. He was subsequently assigned to the 14th Kokutai, a land-based unit stationed in South China, in November 1939 to fly the Mitsubishi A5M Type 96 Carrier Fighter. In January 1940 Kodaira claimed two victories against Chinese Air Force I-15 and I-16 fighters in an attack on Kweilin.

After service in French Indochina, Kodaira returned to Japan in October 1940 to serve with the Omura Kokutai, a training unit for carrier pilots. He was posted to the carrier *Shokaku* in April 1942 and participated in the battles of the Coral Sea and Santa Cruz, claiming one SBD shot down during the latter campaign. In early 1944, Kodaira joined the 601st Kokutai, which was also assigned to *Shokaku*. At the Battle of the Philippine Sea, he was part of the escort for the carrier airplanes from the 1st Koku Sentai's 1st Carrier Division attacking Task Force 58, claiming two Hellcats shot down during the battle before his own fighter was hit and he was forced to ditch.

Rescued and returned to Japan, Kodaira was transferred to the Sento 164th Hikotai, a carrier fighter unit assigned to the 653rd Kokutai. He was on board the carrier *Chitose* during the Battle of Leyte Gulf on October 24, 1944, claiming a Hellcat shot down in the fighting. After *Chitose* was sunk the next day, Kodaira's unit moved to Luzon and participated in operations in the defense of Leyte, flying out of Clark Field. Kodaira was injured in a takeoff accident on November 8 and evacuated to Japan, ending the war with the Sento 304th Hikotai, part of the 252nd Kokutai. He had claimed 11 aerial victories and participated in four carrier battles. Post-war, Kodaira joined the Japanese Air Self-Defense Force. He is believed to still be alive in 2014.

(via Henry Sakaida)

West Coast during the summer of 1943 practiced the "Thach Weave" until it became second nature before they left for combat in the Pacific.

The "Thach Weave" followed the fundamental defensive principle of turning into the enemy's attack, regardless of the direction of the enemy's approach, in close coordination between leader and wingman. The objective of the "Thach Weave" was to disrupt the enemy's attack while putting one of the section's airplanes in a position to fire on the attacker. The "Thach Weave" worked just as well with a division of four aircraft as it did for a section of two.

The US Navy's emphasis, however, was offensive. "The fighter pilot", its booklet on defensive tactics stated, "whose primary mission is the destruction of enemy aircraft, doesn't belong on the defensive". As with defensive tactics, the US Navy endeavored to instill a system of offensive tactics against enemy fighters that would become second nature to a pilot through constant practice. Its offensive tactics were based on three fundamental principles encapsulated as a simple "A-B-C" as follows:

A – Altitude advantage: gain and maintain it.
B – Bracket the enemy and shoot from behind.
C – Combat concentration: attack the enemy with more than one airplane.

With regard to altitude, the US Navy's precepts were simple – attack with an altitude advantage and maintain it. "Altitude is your wealth", the US Navy taught its pilots. "Never spend it unless it buys you speed or an advantageous firing position". Ideally, an attack would begin from an altitude about 2,000ft higher than the enemy fighter, the pilot using the speed he had built up when diving in pursuit of his quarry to climb back up to altitude or to break away. The basic approaches – overhead, side, stern, and head-on – were the same as the basic gunnery approaches learned in training. The US Navy stressed getting in fast, hitting hard with a short burst of fire aimed at the most vulnerable part of the enemy fighter, and making a fast break away.

As with defensive tactics, Naval Aviators were taught the importance of teamwork in the offense as well. To be successful a section had to work as a team using the fundamental "A-B-C" principles, ideally applied to a single enemy aircraft at a time. The section flew and fought as a unit, not as two separate airplanes. Two airplanes, working together, had a better chance of bracketing an enemy fighter and creating an opportunity to get behind the enemy. The same basic system applied to a division of four airplanes, who could divide into two sections to employ the same "A-B-C" principles. Offensive tactics emphasized the necessity of maintaining an altitude advantage and combat concentration in order to facilitate tactical control during the attack. When attacking an enemy formation, a section or division was to attack the highest-flying enemy aircraft first so as to destroy or scatter them, and only then go after enemy airplanes at a lower altitude. On no account was an individual pilot to break formation, as this would hinder his leader's ability to exercise tactical control.

When properly applied these tactics, and a sound foundation in aerial gunnery, gave US Navy pilots an excellent chance of overcoming an enemy fighter. Pilots had to guard against carelessness and complacency. Failure to follow the basic tactical principles, maintain formation discipline or relax alertness could lead to trouble. New fighter pilots were enjoined not to become overconfident. As the tactics booklet stated,

Young IJNAF fighter pilots go over fighter tactics using models of the Zero-sen. Note that the attacking airplane is using the advantage of altitude to dive down on its intended victim. (Author's collection)

"remember that any edge you have on the enemy in the performance, construction and firepower of your airplane will pay off *only* in proportion to your ability to make use of them".

Cdr David McCampbell, the highest scoring Hellcat pilot against the Zero-sen, treated his opponents with a degree of respect. In a post-war interview he said, "I viewed all enemy pilots as equal, because you could never know when you might run into a real topnotch fighter pilot. I always gave my opponent the benefit of the doubt of being a good pilot, and I engaged him in that fashion. I expected him to give his best, and I gave my best."

IJNAF FIGHTER TACTICS

The arrival of the F6F Hellcat in combat presented the IJNAF's Zero-sen pilots with a formidable opponent. With nearly double the horsepower of the A6M, the Hellcat had a speed advantage at all altitudes, and a superior rate of climb above 14,000ft, while its greater weight made it faster in a dive. And although the Zero-sen remained more maneuverable than the Hellcat, especially at lower speeds, the margin of its superiority was not as great as it was over other Allied fighters – at higher speeds the Hellcat could follow the Zero-sen through some maneuvers. Even worse, Hellcat pilots had been trained to avoid the close-in maneuvering combat where the Zero-sen excelled.

The dive, shoot and climb tactics the Hellcat pilots adopted were difficult for the Zero-sen to counter, while even a short burst from the Hellcat's battery of six 0.50in. machine guns was often fatal to a Zero-sen. As one A6M pilot who survived the war recalled, "even if you were an ace or an experienced pilot, without the right strategy it would be useless to fight against a Grumman".

The US Navy based its offensive tactics on three fundamental principles, as illustrated in this diagram of a division of four F6Fs attacking a Japanese formation by sections. The US Navy stressed A) Altitude advantage; B) Bracketing the enemy from either side; and C) Combat concentration, attacking with more than one airplane, section or division to maximize the fire power brought against the enemy. Teamwork was essential, using the section of two airplanes as the basic fighting unit and building this into multiple division attacks as the tactical situation dictated.

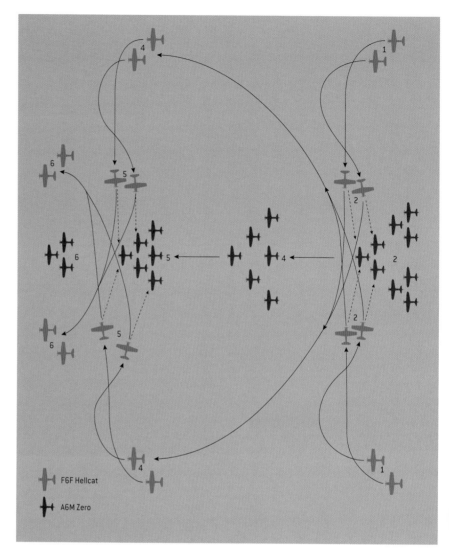

The IJNAF's basic fighting unit was the shotai – three airplanes in a V-formation. This was a loose formation with the two wingmen flying behind the shotai leader at different altitudes. In an attack, the shotai leader could call for successive individual passes in line astern or line abreast, or have one or more of the wingmen remain above as protection or to counter an enemy aircraft's attempt to maneuver away from the attack. When possible, Zero-sen pilots sought an altitude advantage, diving on an enemy aircraft and pulling out below and ahead after their firing run. In maneuvering combat, the Zero-sen pilot would maneuver to deliver a killing burst of fire from close range.

Defensively, the shotai provided mutual support by employing the Zero-sen's superlative maneuverability to quickly turn on an attacking aircraft. When attacked from the rear, the shotai leader could pull up in a tight loop, using the hineri-komi twisting maneuver to come back down on his opponent's tail. The two wingmen would simultaneously execute chandelles to the right and to the left and then a stall turn to catch the enemy fighter from behind.

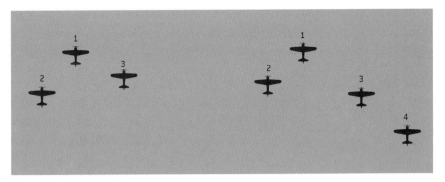

Against the Hellcat, these standard tactics were not always effective. The Zero-sen was superior to the Hellcat in horizontal combat, but not always in the vertical. The opportunities for combat in the horizontal plane were fleeting, and the US Navy's tactic of flying in coordinated sections meant that when a Zero-sen pilot attacked the first Hellcat in a section, the second Hellcat would immediately come to his aid. The danger the US Navy's section tactics posed was even more pronounced when the Zero-sen pilot tried to use a loop to get behind an attacking Hellcat. This maneuver would expose the belly of his airplane to the Hellcat's wingman, and often resulted in a fatal strike.

The best chance a Zero-sen had of shooting down a Hellcat was to catch an American fighter unawares or out of formation. A6M formations would sometimes resort to sending a single airplane down as a decoy to draw an over-eager Hellcat pilot away from his division. Even if a Zero-sen pilot could close with a Hellcat, there was no certain victory as the F6F could absorb a lot of punishment. Zero-sen pilots noted how the Hellcats seemed to simply absorb 7.7mm fire without faltering, while even six 20mm hits were not enough to bring down the big Grumman fighter. The Type 99-2 20mm cannon had a slow firing speed and could not deliver many shells in a single burst.

To hit a vulnerable part of an enemy aircraft, a pilot had to aim carefully. At the beginning of the war many Zero-sen pilots were excellent shots, but as less well-trained pilots reached the front the standard of gunnery steadily declined, making it even harder to shoot down an enemy fighter. To escape an attack, individual Zero-sen pilots often resorted to a split-S, particularly at low altitude where a Hellcat could not follow. Tight horizontal and climbing turns, rolls and chandelles were also frequently employed in combat.

More critical to the survival of Zero-sen pilots in combat with the Hellcat was the IJNAF's comparative lack of coordinated defensive tactics – the lack of adequate radio communication was a great handicap in this regard. The IJNAF failed to develop a tactical system of mutual support comparable to the US Navy's section and division tactics. It was late to adopt the two-element, four-airplane formation of most other air forces, continuing to use the three-airplane shotai formation well into 1944. Even after switching to the four-airplane formation, pilots would break up when engaged and resort to fighting individual combats, rather than mount a coordinated defense.

With some exceptions, where Zero-sen pilots fought effectively in concert, most remained focused on maneuvering in single combat. Individual pilot skill rather than teamwork was still seen as the only way to defeat the enemy. This was perhaps a reflection of the societal tradition of single combat, employing the very "lone wolf" tactics that the US Navy actively discouraged. US Navy Hellcat squadron After Action Reports often referred to Zero-sen formations failing to exercise teamwork or maintain air discipline once attacked.

THE EARLY CLASHES

It is ironic that the first clashes between the premier carrier fighters of the Imperial Japanese and US navies should have been between land-based units in the Solomon Islands. On August 27, 1943, US Navy squadron VF-33 arrived on Guadalcanal with its F6F-3 Hellcats to support the air offensive against Japanese bases on Bougainville and Rabaul. Ten days later, on September 6, 1943, Ens James A. Warren became the first Hellcat pilot to claim a Zero-sen in aerial combat while acting as escort to a formation of TBF Avengers.

A week later, VF-38 and VF-40 brought their Hellcats to Guadalcanal, going into action the next day (14 September) escorting SBDs and TBFs to bomb Ballale airfield on Bougainville. That day VF-33 sent off 16 Hellcats as part of the escort, and Naval Aviators flying these machines claimed eight "Zekes" shot down for the loss of one Hellcat (whose wounded pilot made a water landing just off the airfield at Munda) and another damaged in a belly landing at Munda airfield.

During the mission Lt Carlos Hildebrandt claimed three "Zekes" shot down, knocking the first one off the tail of another Hellcat. "I poured lead into him", Hildebrandt told the squadron intelligence officer on his return, "and he rolled over on his back smoking at 200ft. Tracers went by me then, so I pulled up sharply and collected 7.7mm slugs through the canopy. They went into my jungle pack and my back. The Zero turned away as I turned into Fruin [his wingman, who had a "Zeke" following him]. Firing from 100 yards, I continued through his pullout and roll. He went in when his port wing was shot off. Then I was jumped at 100ft by a "Zeke". Using the hand lever to dump my flaps, I saw the Jap go by and pull up in a turn. I just held the trigger down until he blew up."

The Zero-sen pilots flying in the Solomons were used to fighting with the F4U Corsair and the P-38 Lightning, so the arrival of the Hellcat did not make as big an impression as it did in the first encounters in the Central Pacific.

To give his new carrier force some combat experience, and a chance to work out carrier doctrine, Adm Nimitz authorized a series of hit-and-run raids on Japanese bases. The first two raids, against Marcus Island on August 31, 1943 and Tarawa on September 18, failed to encounter any IJNAF fighters, but the third strike, against Wake Island on October 5, did. The pilots of the 252nd Kokutai, defending the island, lost 16 Zero-sen fighters to the 48 marauding Hellcats of VF-5, VF-9, VF-16 and VF-25, who claimed 30 "Zekes" shot down in the early morning attack.

VF-33 was the first squadron to take the F6F Hellcat into combat, and the first to claim a victory over a Zero-sen. VF-38 and VF-40 soon joined it in the Solomons, flying out of Guadalcanal and then the airfield at Munda, on the island of New Georgia. (Robert Lawson Collection, National Naval Aviation Museum)

The pilots of VF-16 after the combats of November 23–24, 1943. Lt(jg) Eugene Hanks stands in the center, holding up five fingers representing his claims for five Zero-sens shot down on the 23rd. (80G-205408, RG80, NARA)

This raid demonstrated the Hellcat's superiority over the Zero-sen, despite the latter's ability to turn inside the Hellcat. All the combats took place below 12,000ft, the F6F proving to be faster than the Zero-sen and demonstrating its ability to outrun its Japanese opponent. Although the Zero-sen showed a better rate of climb at these altitudes, in several combats where the IJNAF fighter initiated a climbing turn to evade an attacking Hellcat, the latter was able to follow the Zero-sen in the turn and shoot it down. The Hellcat pilots noted that the gunnery of their IJNAF counterparts was poor, and that, with one exception, they acted as single airplanes and not as teams. The Hellcat pilots returned to their carriers full of enthusiasm for their new fighter.

The next significant clashes between the Hellcat and the Zero-sen took place over Rabaul during two successive carrier strikes in early November 1943. On the 5th, *Saratoga* and *Princeton*, as Task Force 38, launched a strike against shipping in Rabaul harbor, with fighter cover provided by land-based F6F units from Vella Lavella. Hellcat pilots from VF-12 and VF-23 ran into Zero-sens from the 1st Koku Sentai (Air Flotilla) (*Zuikaku*, *Shokaku* and *Zuiho* air groups) and the 11th Koku Kantai (Air Fleet) (201st, 204th, 251st and 253rd Kokutais), claiming 17 "Zekes" destroyed. Six days later a combined force from Task Force 38 and Task Group 50.3, which included the aircraft carriers *Essex*, USS *Bunker Hill* (CV-17) and *Independence*, went back to attack Rabaul harbor. In the ensuing combats Hellcat pilots from VF-9, VF-18 and VF-22 claimed an

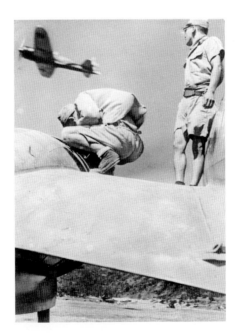

A Zero-sen takes off from an airfield on Rabaul as a groundcrewman working on a Type 1 Navy Attack Bomber ("Betty") turns to watch. (via the author)

All models of the A6M Zero-sen were equipped with the Navy Type 98 reflector gunsight. Based on the German Revi 2b, the Type 98 gunsight featured a circular reticle pattern. It replaced earlier model telescopic gunsights, going into production shortly after the A6M2 Model 21 Zero-sen entered service. Unlike their American counterparts, the IJN and JAAF developed their own gunsights and other equipment – a seemingly unnecessary duplication of effort.

In combat with the Hellcat, and other second-generation American fighters, Zero-sen pilots found the armament of two 7.7mm machine guns and two slow-firing 20mm cannon to be less than adequate. US Navy tactics and the Hellcat's superior performance gave Zero-sen pilots little time to get in a killing burst of fire. The Type 99 7.7mm machine guns had little effect on a Hellcat, and using the Type 99 20mm cannon effectively required skilled gunnery. However, with

the quality of pilot training declining as the war went on, the gunnery skills of newly operational pilots dropped off markedly. Many Zero-sen pilots would have preferred a battery of faster-firing 13.2mm machine guns. Indeed, a solitary example of this weapon was installed in the A6M5b Model 52b in place of the right-hand Type 97 7.7mm gun, although its introduction meant that the pilot of the aircraft now had three different shell trajectories to deal with!

From US Navy After Action Reports and memoirs of surviving Japanese pilots, it appears that the Zero-sen pilot's best chance of downing a Hellcat was to come in on the US Navy fighter unseen and fire from close range at its fuel tanks in the wings (there are several reports of Hellcats going down in flames after being hit in this area) or other vital areas with the 20mm cannon.

additional 29 "Zekes" destroyed while escorting the attacking force of SBDs and TBFs.

On November 23 the US Navy launched the invasion of the Gilbert Islands, landing US Army troops on Makin and Marines on Tarawa. Flying off *Lexington* in support of the invasion, VF-16 claimed 25 "Zekes" shot down on November 23–24. During the combats on the 23rd Lt(jg) Eugene Hanks became the first Hellcat pilot to claim five "Zekes" destroyed in a single mission. A newly appointed division leader, Hanks led his division down in an attack on a formation of Zero-sens that had scattered after an earlier attack, boring in on a shotai of three aircraft and exploding one that he identified as a "Hamp" (A6M3 Model 32). He quickly shot down two more "Hamps", and got two "Zekes" as well before he ran out of ammunition. The next day his squadron colleague Lt(jg) Alfred Frendberg claimed his fifth "Zeke", becoming the second Hellcat pilot to become an ace against the Zero-sen.

After the capture of the Gilberts, Task Force 50, with four *Essex* class and two *Independence* class carriers assigned, raided Kwajalein, in the Marshall Islands, VF-2, VF-5, VF-9, VF-16 and VF-25 claiming 33 "Zekes" shot down. The 1st Koku Sentai lost six Zero-sens and 281st Kokutai records indicate that it had ten destroyed.

A Zero-sen goes down in flames, both wings on fire. Lacking armored protection for the fuel tanks installed near the wing roots, the Zero-sen burned easily. Hellcat pilots learned to aim for the fuel tanks, which were the A6M's most vulnerable points. (80G-46982, RG80, NARA)

By the end of 1943, carrier-based Hellcats had claimed 148 Japanese fighters (principally Zero-sens) shot down, while their land-based colleagues in the Solomons had been credited with a further 59 fighters, for a combined loss of 35 Hellcats in aerial combat against Japanese bombers and fighters.

It was now possible to draw some conclusions about the relative performance of the two airplanes. Most pilots agreed that the Zero-sen was clearly superior to the Hellcat in turns at low speed and in aerobatic maneuvers, but at higher speeds Hellcat pilots could match a Zero-sen through most of a turn. The Hellcat had the edge in level and diving speeds, and could often out-climb the Zero-sen at low and medium altitudes. This gave Hellcat pilots the great benefit of being able to maintain an altitude advantage over their IJNAF foes.

In its After Action Report for the mission of December 4, 1943, VF-16 commented that "as far as armament, armor and general ruggedness of the airplanes were concerned, the F6F again showed itself immeasurably superior to the Zero". Of the 19 "Zekes" the squadron claimed shot down in combat that day, for the loss of one Hellcat, 16 either blew up or went down on fire. In contrast, the Hellcat proved capable of taking a great deal of punishment. One F6F-3 returned to the carrier with more than 200 holes from anti-aircraft fire and 7.7mm and 20mm fire from an attacking Zero-sen that had peppered the wings and fuselage, destroyed the radio and knocked off half the right horizontal stabilizer.

The Zero-sen pilots were having a difficult time coping with the Hellcat, as the relative losses indicate. Although there was clearly some over-claiming by both sides in the heat of combat, the Zero-sen units were losing more pilots and airplanes than they could afford to to the Hellcats they were encountering in increasing numbers. Years later, one former Zero-sen pilot likened the Hellcat to a wild boar with razor-sharp tusks and the Zero-sen to a refined city girl, commenting that "you don't

Lt(jg) Marvin Franger of VF-9 shows how he followed and shot down a Zero-sen as it pulled up in a loop during the attack on Roi, in Kwajalein, on January 29, 1944. (80G-217501, RG80, NARA)

send out a refined city girl to fight a wild boar with sharp tusks".

According to accounts being sent back from Hellcat pilots in the frontline, the level of opposition they were encountering when engaging Zero-sens in combat depended on how experienced their foes were.

In one particular clash over Kwajalein, an F6F squadron ran into a group of Zero-sen pilots who the Hellcat formation leader found were "a first-line team that knew what they were doing. Six Zeros positioned themselves on each section, with two always firing at each section. When we headed towards them, they would immediately straighten up, make a violent pull out and go up at a 60-degree angle. The two firing airplanes were immediately replaced by two more feeding down from the center. Three or four reversals resulted in their using two firing airplanes to hit us in the turns and immediately pull out as soon as we could open fire on them. Two of their firing airplanes shot at us from the *outside* of their turns". The squadron lost a Hellcat in the combat before breaking away and making its escape, but as the formation leader admitted, "Why they didn't shoot all of us down is more than I can figure out. They certainly had ample opportunity, and no doubt would have done it if they had been more proficient gunners".

TRUK AND PALAU

Ens Isamu Miyazaki of the 252nd Kokutai was a chivalrous pilot who spared the life of an opponent flying a badly damaged F6F-3 on January 30, 1944. Forlornly trying to defend the Marshall Islands, Miyazaki and three other pilots from the 252nd fought an uneven dogfight that saw three Zero-sens sustain damage and withdraw. Now alone, Miyazaki spotted a solitary damaged Hellcat flying just above the sea. He tailed the American fighter until satisfied that his opponent could not fight. Flying alongside the F6F, Miyazaki stared at the pilot, who "had such a pitiful expression on his face", the IJNAF ace later recalled, that "I didn't have the heart to shoot him down, so I let him go". Ens Fletcher Jones of VF-10 eventually ditched his fighter, but was drowned. Miyazaki, however, survived the war with 13 victories to his name. (Isamu Miyazaki)

In the first few months of 1944 the IJNAF suffered further blows from a mounting Allied offensive. At the end of January, the Fast Carrier Task Force, now designated Task Force 58 under the command of Rear Adm Marc Mitscher, covered the invasion of the Marshall Islands and the capture of Kwajalein and Roi. Allied airplanes continued to hammer at Rabaul, the Hellcats of VF-33, VF-38 and VF-40 contributing claims of 46 Zero-sens destroyed. But the worst blow fell on February 17, when Task Force 58 launched a devastating raid on the IJN's bastion at Truk. It was defended by elements of the 201st, 204th, 251st, 501st and 902nd Kokutais.

By coincidence, a few days before the American attack the IJNAF had flown in a large number of new A6M5 Model 52 Zero-sens to Truk, some of them being earmarked as reinforcements for the units still fighting on Rabaul. The newly arrived replacement pilots and combat veterans from Rabaul began training intensively, but they soon learned that an America force was on its way.

In the early hours of February 17, Mitscher despatched 72 Hellcats on a fighter sweep to

knock out Japanese fighters, before sending in the dive- and torpedo-bombers. The Zero-sen units rose to meet the American aircraft, and a swirling dogfight followed. Noritsura Kotaka, an A6M pilot who survived the day, recalled looking up and seeing more than 150 Hellcats and Zero-sens above him in a huge aerial battle, with many airplanes going down in flames and fires everywhere from airfields under attack.

Kotaka, who had taken off with three other Zero-sens, found himself coming in behind two Hellcats. One broke to the right in front of him. Pressing in to very close range he opened fire, hitting the Hellcat in the wings and sending it spinning down. However, he forgot about the other Hellcat. In an instant the second fighter was behind him, firing. Kotaka broke down and to the right, but the Hellcat easily followed his maneuver, hitting his airplane with a burst of fire and sending it straight down towards the sea. Kotaka, having barely managed to pull out, climbed back up and found another Hellcat in front of him, hitting it and sending it down too. While trying to get back to his base, Kotaka was attacked by yet another Hellcat. His airplane was hit for a second time, which damaged its controls. Nevertheless, Kotaka miraculously survived this second attack, and on landing he counted 26 bullet holes in his Zero-sen.

Many of his compatriots were not so fortunate. The Hellcats from VF-5, VF-6, VF-9, VF-10 and VF-18 claimed 62 "Zekes" destroyed for the loss of two Hellcats in aerial combat – five F6F pilots claimed three "Zekes" apiece. The actual number of Zero-sens shot down was less than the number claimed, but the losses were devastating nonetheless. The 204th Kokutai was decimated, losing 18 pilots killed out of 31 sent off. In addition, many more Zero-sens and other Japanese aircraft were destroyed on the ground.

Over the next three months Task Force 58 ranged far and wide across the Pacific striking at Japanese bases. The most intense combat took place during attacks on the Palau Islands on March 30–31, 1944. Mitscher again sent in 72 Hellcats on a fighter

A Zero-sen under attack over Truk on February 17, 1944. The Hellcat squadrons claimed 62 A6Ms shot down in the attacks on Truk. (80G-476109, RG80, NARA)

RIGHT
A "Zeke" goes down in flames during the attack on Palau on March 30–31, 1944. Several of the attacking Hellcat squadrons noted the lack of coordinated defensive tactics on the part of their opponents during these one-sided clashes. (80G-476108, RG80, NARA)

sweep over the target area. Hellcats from VF-5, VF-8, VF-23 and VF-30 ran into 20 Zero-sens from the 201st Kokutai and 12 from the Sento 351st Hikotai, a fighter-bomber unit from the 501st Kokutai. The American pilots claimed 22 "Zekes" and, oddly, three Army Type 1 Fighters ("Oscars") shot down. The Zero-sen units lost 14 airplanes shot down and two more to force-landings – every surviving airplane also received damage.

Later that day 52 Zero-sens from the 261st and 263rd Kokutais flew in to Palau as reinforcements, engaging the Hellcats on March 31 in more fierce combats over the islands. The 261st lost 20 Zero-sens shot down, four more badly damaged, and another four destroyed in strafing attacks, wiping out the unit, while the 263rd lost 15 aircraft shot down and two destroyed on the ground. The Hellcat pilots claimed 56 fighters destroyed, all for the loss of three F6Fs in aerial combat over the two-day battle. The Japanese pilots appeared to be inexperienced. The attacking VF-5 pilots observed the Zero-sens flying in four-airplane flights, but once combat was joined the Japanese pilots rarely provided tactical support to each other. Additionally, Naval Aviators from VF-30 commented on the A6M pilots' lack of aggressiveness and apparent inability to make the best use of the Zero-sen's maneuverability and superior rate of climb.

THE MARIANAS

As is well known, the Battle of the Philippine Sea in June 1944 ended in defeat for the IJN. It had made preparations for Operation *A-Go* (the defense of the Marianas) in expectation of the American assault. The IJN's carrier air groups had been reorganized and equipped with new-production A6M5b Zero-sens, but the majority of the pilots assigned to fly them into action were fresh out of training with limited flying hours – only a small core of experienced pilots remained to guide them in battle.

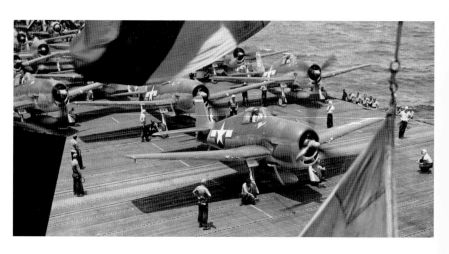

Cdr David McCampbell, CVG-15 commander, about to take off from *Essex* in his F6F-3 *The Minisi* in June 1944. McCampbell claimed 4.5 Zero-sens shot down during the battles over the Marianas. (80G-469996, RG80, NARA)

The fighting began on June 11 when Task Force 58 launched strikes against all the Marianas Islands, and lasted until the attack on the Japanese fleet on June 20. During the nine days of fighting around the islands, and later over Iwo Jima, the Hellcat squadrons of Task Force 58 claimed 371 Zero-sens shot down – 217 on June 19 alone, the day of the "Great Marianas Turkey Shoot". The experienced IJNAF pilots who survived the battle noted that the Hellcat pilots they encountered appeared more aggressive and more confident in fighting against the Zero-sen. The American Naval Aviators brought to the battle months of training, superior tactics and combat experience that enabled them to get more out of their fighters than their Japanese opponents could.

Pilots of VF-2 on board *Hornet* prepare to depart on a mission over the Marianas during June 1944. Note the three different styles of national marking on the sides of the fuselage of these F6F-3s. (80G-469191, RG80, NARA)

An indication of the dominance the Hellcat pilots exercised during the battle can be found in the number of aviators with multiple Zero-sen claims in a single day, or combat. During the battle one Hellcat pilot claimed five "Zekes" shot down, six pilots claimed four and 20 pilots claimed three apiece. Many of the Hellcats involved were late model F6F-3s, which boasted water injection for added power that enabled the pilots to fight more effectively. Indeed, they always attacked from higher altitude.

While some Hellcat squadrons encountered groups of well-flown Zero-sens, others found that many of their Japanese opponents employed tactics that VF-2 noted were "erratic and disorganized". Time after time a Zero-sen would explode or burst into flames when under fire from a Hellcat, while the Hellcat pilots found the Zero-sen's 7.7mm weapons to be "virtually ineffectual against the F6F, and the 20mm has such a low muzzle velocity that many of our air group's airplanes have returned with holes in their wings and fuselage without serious impediment to flight operations".

The campaign for the Marianas and subsequent strikes on the Bonin Islands saw the combat debut of the F6F-5 model of the Hellcat. VF-13, one of the first squadrons to take the "Dash Five" into action, noted the improvement in maximum and diving speeds and superior maneuverability in a dive over the F6F-3, although the F6F-5 was still unable to turn with a "Zeke" at low speeds. This variant was also fitted with water injection.

VF-13 and VF-2, who first used the "Dash Five" in the strikes on

Veteran pilots of the Yokosuka Kokutai (the oldest land-based unit in the IJNAF, having been formed on April 1, 1916) fought an overwhelming number of Hellcats over Iwo Jima during June–July 1944. The unit had sent 51 Zero-sens to defend the Bonin Islands as part of the *A-Go* operation, and although its pilots subsequently claimed ten Hellcats destroyed and six more as probables, these successes came at a high cost. Indeed, by July 4 the Kokutai had no airworthy fighters left. The aces amongst these pilots are WO Ryoji Oh-hara (16 kills, front row, left), Ens Masami Shiga (16 kills, back row, second from left), WOs Tomita Atake (ten victories, back row, third from left) and Kiyoshi Sekiya (11 kills, back row, second from right). (Yasuho Izawa)

the Bonins in early July, found that the F6F-5 could outrun a "Zeke" at any altitude, and could match its rate of climb. Even with the improved F6F-5, the Zero-sen in the hands of experienced pilots could still prove dangerous, however. During the July 3 fighter sweep over Iwo Jima, in the Bonin Islands, VF-2 ran into a group of veteran pilots from the 252nd Kokutai and the Sento 601st Hikotai. While the Hellcat pilots claimed 33 Zero-sens shot down, the squadron lost four aircraft and two pilots. Three of the Japanese veterans, who claimed 13 Hellcats shot down between them on July 3, were shot down and killed the next day in combat with another force of Hellcats.

THE PHILIPPINES CAMPAIGN

Following the disastrous Marianas battle, the IJNAF reorganized its aviation units, disbanding those decimated in recent combats and absorbing the remaining pilots into others. Units were brought back up to strength in aircraft numbers through new production, but there was a critical shortage of experienced pilots and combat leaders. In some units, the majority of pilots were classed as barely operational, able to fly their aircraft but lacking adequate training in combat tactics and gunnery.

As to aircraft, the A6M5 remained the mainstay of the IJNAF's fighter Kokutai. By the end of August 1944, the Kawanishi Kokuki K.K. had produced only 521 of its advanced N1K1-J fighters and just seven improved N1K2-J – in contrast, Grumman was producing more than 500 Hellcats a month. The IJNAF's 1st, 2nd and 3rd Koku Kantai (its main force) had around 700 to 750 fighters with a serviceability rate of between 50 and 60 percent. Knowing that the defense of the Philippines was vital to Japan's survival, the IJNAF assigned the majority of its fighter squadrons to this task.

In contrast, the air groups of the US Navy's Fast Carrier Task Force (which became Task Force 38 on shifting to Adm Halsey's Third Fleet command) were rapidly re-equipping with the F6F-5 Hellcat. In August 1944 the US Navy changed the composition of its carrier air groups, increasing the complement of fighter squadrons to 54 aircraft by reducing the number of dive-bombers from 36 to 24. Task Force 38 now had nine *Essex* class and eight *Independence* class carriers with some 560 Hellcats (including photo-airplanes and nightfighters) embarked. An efficient logistical system brought a steady stream of replacement aircraft to the fleet.

In mid-September Task Force 38 launched a series of strikes against Japanese air bases in the Philippines. Over four days, the Hellcat squadrons claimed 94 Zero-sens shot down. The relative

F6F-5 Hellcats of VF-11 prepare to take off from the *Hornet* for the October 10, 1944 strike on the Nansei Shoto islands north of Okinawa. Note that several of the fighters are carrying a full load of six HVAR rockets under the wings. (80G-284460, RG80, NARA)

lack of Japanese resistance brought a change of plans, bringing forward the invasion of the Philippines to October 20, 1944 with landings on Leyte.

The Fast Carrier Task Force was charged with reducing Japanese air strength on Formosa and Luzon in preparation for the amphibious assault. During three days of strikes on Formosa, on October 12, 13 and 14, the Hellcat squadrons claimed 107 Zero-sens shot down from a total of 353 Japanese aircraft destroyed, with 85 "Zeke" claims on the first day of the strikes – the second highest daily total of

A VF-29 F6F-3 takes off from USS *Cabot* (CVL-28) in October 1944, while an F6F-5 waits to move forward. At this time the F6F-5 was replacing the F6F-3 within fleet Hellcat squadrons. (80G-286529, RG80, NARA)

the war against the Zero-sen. Shifting back to the Philippines, four days of strikes brought additional claims of 80 Zero-sens.

Over the next two months, Task Force 38 provided support for the landings on Leyte, Mindoro and Luzon. In aerial battles with IJNAF and Japanese Army Air Force (JAAF) fighters during the campaign for the Philippines, the Fast Carriers claimed more than 900 aircraft shot down and hundreds more destroyed on the ground. From the date of the landings on Leyte to the end of 1944, the Hellcat squadrons were credited with an additional 233 Zero-sens shot down.

There is no better evidence of the dominance of the Hellcat over the Zero-sen by this stage of the war than Cdr David McCampbell's famous mission of October 24, 1944 when he and his wingman, Lt(jg) Roy Rushing, claimed 12 Zero-sens between them. They were the highest scorers during a day that saw Hellcat pilots claim another 74 Zero-sens shot down. One other F6F pilot claimed five Zero-sens shot down, another got four, and four others claimed three each. The experience of one young ensign flying as part of a division from VF-19 that day is indicative of the confidence Hellcat pilots had in their airplane, their tactics and their training. Ens George McPherson, who had shared in the destruction of a JAAF Type 3 Fighter ("Tony") 12 days previously, shot down a "Zeke" for his last claim of the war. In the VF-19 After Action Report McPherson said:

I spotted three "Zekes", turned toward them and gave a tallyho report. One "Zeke" started a gentle right turn, one split-essed and one started a level right turn. I picked the one in the climbing turn, closing at 230–240 knots. At my first burst he tightened his turn rapidly. I did likewise and hit with my second burst. The plane exploded as he went into the cloud.

Two weeks later VF-19 engaged a mixed formation of JAAF and IJNAF fighters over Manila, claiming 13 destroyed. Reflecting the rapidly declining quality of the Japanese pilot force in the Philippines, the After Action Report commented that

Cdr David McCampbell lands his F6F-5 *Minsi III* after his historic mission of October 24, 1944, when he and his wingman Lt(jg) Roy Rushing claimed 15 Japanese fighters destroyed between them. (80G-258180, RG80, NARA)

"enemy airplanes were fast but not fast enough. They did not attempt to outmaneuver us but made slow jinking turns and were helpful in their own destruction through lack of teamwork and head work".

In the intense combat over the Philippines, many IJNAF fighter units were annihilated. Reinforcing squadrons fed in as replacements met the same fate. Aerial combat fell off markedly after the first week of December, the Hellcat squadrons claiming only 16 Zero-sens during the last half of the month. Seeing no alternative way to strike back at American naval forces with any remote chance of success, the Japanese high command turned to the Tokubetsu Kogekitai – the infamous Special Attack units that would tragically consume hundreds of Zero-sens and their young pilots until the end of the war.

An F6F-5 of VF-7 armed with four HVAR rockets takes off from USS *Hancock* (CV-19) on a strike against targets in the Philippines in December 1944. By this stage of the war the Hellcat was regularly employed as a fighter-bomber. (80G-259020, RG80, NARA)

STATISTICS AND ANALYSIS

From their first clash on October 5, 1943 until the end of 1944, US Navy Hellcat pilots claimed approximately 1,540 A6M Zero-sen fighters of all models shot down. During that same period, the US Navy lost 167 carrier-based and 23 land-based Hellcats in aerial combat, although not all fell in combat with the Zero-sen, as the Hellcat squadrons engaged other Japanese fighter and bomber types as well.

Not surprisingly, the victory-to-loss ratio always favored the Hellcat, but varied over time and combat area. The land-based Hellcat units fighting in the Solomons during 1943 had a victory-to-loss ratio against all Japanese aircraft (although 83 percent of the airplanes they shot down were fighters) of 4.2-to-1. On most of their missions in the Solomons, the Hellcat squadrons acted as escorts for the bombers, and often did not have an altitude advantage over the Zero-sen pilots they encountered. Another factor may have been that the IJNAF units they fought against had greater experience fighting more powerful American fighters than the Zero-sen units in the Central Pacific at this time. The ratio for land-based Hellcat units did improve to 10.8-to-1 during 1944.

In contrast, the carrier-based Hellcats put up a 13.9-to-1 ratio against all types of Japanese aircraft (of which 59 percent were

An A6M5 Model 52 in flight over Japan, with Mount Fuji in the background. Zero-sen units were active in the defense of Japan and over Okinawa, but many were also held in reserve waiting for the expected American invasion. (Australian War Memorial 129698-1)

By 1945 Grumman was turning out hundreds of F6F-5s each month. An efficient logistical system maintained a steady flow of replacement aircraft to the Fleet. Production ended in November 1945. (Robert Lawson Collection, National Naval Aviation Museum)

fighters) during 1943. For the first four months of 1944, when Task Force 58 made repeated surprise raids on Japanese bases in the Central Pacific, the ratio climbed to 22-to-1. Hellcat losses in air combat mounted during the second half of the year in the fierce combats over the Marianas, Iwo Jima, Formosa and the Philippines, but the Hellcat maintained an overall victory-to-loss ratio of 20-to-1 against all Japanese aircraft (74 percent of which were fighters) for all of 1944, mirroring the decline in IJNAF pilot quality. During the last year of the war, from September 1944 to August 1945, Hellcat pilots established a 13-to-1 victory ratio over the Zero-sen.

Carrier-based Hellcat Claims Against Japanese Aircraft 1943–45

Year	Bombers	Fighters	Hellcat Losses	Victory-to-Loss Ratio
1943	103	148	18	13.9-to-1
1944	774	2,206	149	20.0-to-1
1945	510	1,214	78	22.1-to-1

(Source – Naval Aviation Combat Statistics-World War II)

The Hellcat entered combat a little over a year after the American landing on Guadalcanal. In the intervening months American Marine, Navy, Army Air Force and Allied fighter squadrons waged a relentless war of attrition against the IJNAF over the Solomon Islands and New Guinea, inflicting losses the Japanese could ill afford. From the withdrawal of IJNAF units from Rabaul (and out of the range of Allied land-based fighters) at the end of February 1944, until the return of USAAF fighter squadrons to Leyte at the end of October, the Hellcat squadrons of the Fast Carrier Task Force took over the battle of attrition against the IJNAF, continuing to inflict punishing losses on its fighter units.

More important than the destruction of enemy fighters was the ability of the Hellcat squadrons to clear the air for the strike forces – the dive- and torpedo-bombers that pounded Japanese airfields and military installations and sank vital Japanese shipping. From January 1944 to January 1945, US Navy SBDs, SB2Cs and TBMs dropped a total of 18,699 tons of bombs on Japanese targets and sank more than 100 IJN warships and 200 merchant vessels. During the entire war, the US Navy lost only 82 carrier-based dive- and torpedo-bombers in aerial combat during 60,420 sorties – a loss rate of 0.14 percent.

In breaking the IJNAF's fighter force during 1944, the Hellcats supported the Fast Carrier Task Force's ability to range across the Central Pacific to strike at Japanese bases, destroying some and leaving others isolated, defeating the IJN's plans to create an island barrier against the American fleet. A year after the first carrier strikes on Marcus Island, the fast carriers were attacking the Philippines. With the aid of radar and fighter direction, the Hellcat proved to be equally adept at defending the fleet. In a year of combat, the Fast Carrier Task Force lost only one carrier to air attack – *Princeton*, sunk on October 24, 1944 off the Philippines.

The IJNAF's ranking ace, who personally claimed 202 victories (including 14 in China in 1938), Lt(jg) Tetsuzo Iwamoto survived nearly eight years of frontline service as a fighter pilot. Immune to life-threatening (in a fighter pilot at least) traits like blind spirit and bravado, his favored technique in combat was a vertical diving pass. Iwamoto also knew when to fight and when to run. A veteran of most of the early Pacific War campaigns (flying from the carrier *Zuikaku*), he subsequently served with a series of land-based, Zero-sen-equipped kokutais (204th, 253rd, 252nd and the 203rd) from November 1943 through to the spring of 1945. By war's end Iwamoto had claimed 29 F6F Hellcats shot down in battles over Formosa, the Philippines, Okinawa and in defense of the homeland. (Yasuho Izawa)

As suggested in the Introduction to this volume, the duel between the Hellcat and the Zero-sen reflected a larger battle between rival aeronautical technologies and industrial capacities, a battle America won. It was first to develop powerful aircraft engines of 2,000hp, design new fighters around these engines and get them into quantity production ahead of Japan. The 2,980 Japanese aircraft lost to Hellcats in aerial combat during 1944 was the result. The Japanese aviation industry was never able to catch up, and eventually it ran out of time.

While the Hellcat could out-perform the Zero-sen in most areas except maneuverability, having an aircraft of superior performance was not the sole requirement for success. Pilot quality was equally important. In this area the US Navy did a better job than the IJNAF of providing its pilots with the training and combat tactics they needed to get the most out of their airplane. The US Navy's development of coordinated defensive and offensive tactics, based on teamwork between sections and divisions, and the rigorous practice in these tactics, proved superior to the individual combat tactics employed by the majority of Zero-sen pilots.

It is interesting to note that the victory-to-loss ratio of the Hellcat against the later models of Japanese fighters (the N1J1/2 Shiden and Shiden-Kai ("George"), the J2M Raiden ("Jack") and the Army Type 4 Fighter ("Frank")) was 8.5-to-1 – still in the Hellcat's favor, but a lower ratio than against the Zero-sen. Had these later Japanese fighters been flown by pilots with more training and better tactics, the ratio might well have been worse.

During 1943–44 there were 23 Hellcat pilots who claimed seven or more victories against the Zero-sen, and around another 17 who claimed six victories. The high scorer was Cdr David McCampbell of VF-15, who counted 14.5 Zero-sens among his 34 victories – four other VF-15 pilots were in this top group. VF-2 also had five pilots among the top scorers against the A6M. Of the 23 pilots who claimed seven or more victories, six completed their flight training before the attack on Pearl Harbor, 12 finished during 1942 and four during 1943. Only four pilots had any combat experience prior to going into action with the Hellcat.

While the US Navy's ace pilots feature more prominently in the histories of aerial combat over the Pacific, it is important to note the contribution of the many young Hellcat pilots, like Ens George McPherson, who shot down two, three or even four Zero-sens during their time in combat. These victories were just as damaging cumulatively to the IJNAF and account for the majority of Zero-sens the Hellcats destroyed. Unlike the IJN, in the later years of the war the US Navy did not have to rely on a smaller and smaller cadre of experienced aces – a further confirmation of the quality of the US Navy's training system. A lack of records makes it difficult to identify equivalent IJNAF top scorers against the Hellcat, but its top ace, Lt(jg) Tetsuzo Iwamoto, claimed 29 F6F Hellcats shot down in battles over Formosa, the Philippines, Okinawa and in defense of the homeland, although his actual total is unknown.

Leading A6M Zero-sen Killers of 1943–44			
Aces	Unit(s)	A6M Claims	Total Claims
Cdr David McCampbell	CVG-15	14.5	34
Lt Cecil Harris	VF-27/18	10	24
Cdr William Dean	VF-2	9	11
Lt John Strane	VF-15	9	13
Lt(jg) Roy Rushing	VF-15	9	13
Lt(jg) Robert Carlson	VF-40/30	8.5	9
Lt John Wirth	VF-31	8	14
Lt Cdr George Duncan	VF-15	8	13.5
Lt Hamilton McWhorter	VF-9	8	12
Lt Lloyd Barnard	VF-2	8	9
Lt Cdr Paul Buie	VF-16	8	9
Lt Landis Doner	VF-2	8	8
Lt Richard Eastman	VF-1	8	9
Lt Everett Hargreaves	VF-2	8	8.5
Lt Arthur Van Haren Jr	VF-2	8	9
Lt Cornelius Nooy	VF-31	7	19
Lt(jg) Alexander Vraciu	VF-6/16	7	19
Lt(jg) Wendell Twelves	VF-15	7	13
Lt Robert Duncan	VF-5	7	7
Lt Mayo Hadden	VF-9	7	8
Lt Harry Hill	VF-5	7	7
Lt(jg) Daniel Rehms	VF-50/8	7	9
Ens Frank Schneider (KIA)	VF-33	7	7

AFTERMATH

The Zero-sen fought to the bitter end of the war in defense of the Japanese homeland and in the attempt to defeat the American invasion of Okinawa in April 1945. Many of the remaining IJNAF pilots with experience transferred to units flying the J2M Raiden ("Jack") or the N1K2-J ("George"), but a larger number continued to fly the Zero-sen. These men now faced overwhelming odds.

For the invasion of Okinawa, Task Force 58 marshaled ten fleet carriers (CV) and six light carriers (CVL) with 534 F6F-5 Hellcats and 303 F4U-1/4 Corsairs. The carrier air groups were soon supplemented by land-based US Marine Corps Corsair squadrons and, later, USAAF P-47Ns on Okinawa and P-51Ds flying from Iwo Jima.

By this point in the war the IJNAF was focused almost exclusively on using the Special Attack force to counter the American invasion. The IJNAF's experienced pilots, the equivalent of the Luftwaffe's "Alter Hase" (Old Hares), were employed as

The Zero-sen units fought until the end of the war, the last combats between the Hellcat and the IJNAF fighter taking place on August 15, 1945. This A6M5 Model 52c belonging to the 302nd Kokutai lies forlorn on a Japanese airfield after the surrender. (Jack Lambert Collection, Museum of Flight)

An F6F-5 Hellcat from VF-86 showing two kill markings. On August 15, 1945 Lt(jg) Ora Myers from this unit became the last Hellcat pilot of the war to claim a Zero-sen. (National Museum of Naval Aviation)

escorts to the poorly trained Kamikaze, in more often than not futile attempts to clear a path through the combat air patrols of US Navy and US Marine Corps fighters. With the failure to defeat the American invasion, the IJNAF went on the defensive, hoarding its remaining airplanes for the pending invasion of Japan.

The last combats between the Hellcat and the Zero-sen took place on August 15, 1945. Early that morning a division of four Hellcats from VF-49 off USS *San Jacinto* (CVL-30) and four from VF-31 off *Belleau Wood* were on a sweep of airfields north of Tokyo. Seeing a number of A6Ms attacking a formation of British Fleet Air Arm Avengers, the Hellcats jettisoned their bombs and climbed up after the Japanese fighters. The IJNAF pilots were aggressive, abandoning their attack on the torpedo-bombers to engage the Hellcats, but in uncoordinated runs. VF-49's After Action Report recorded that "our flight was in a weave at the start of the fight, but the Jap airplanes came from every section of the sky, and it soon became a very mixed fight".

The VF-49 pilots found, as had so many of their brethren before them, that the Zero-sen was more maneuverable than the F6F-5, but it burned easily. In the space of a few furious minutes, the four Hellcat pilots claimed seven Zero-sens shot down, two probables and two damaged, while their VF-31 colleagues claimed a further six. Five minutes after the fight ended an announcement came over the radio that Japan had surrendered. That same afternoon Lt(jg) Ora Myers of VF-86, flying off USS *Wasp* (CV-14), encountered a "Zeke" and shot it down – the final engagement in a duel between the Hellcat and the Zero-sen that had lasted nearly two years.

The Mitsubishi A6M8 Model 63 was the last model of the Zero-sen, and the fastest. The IJNAF had finally allowed Mitsubishi to replace the Sakae engine with the more powerful Kinsei, but too late for this improved model to go into production before the war ended. (Peter M. Bowers Collection, Museum of Flight)

The final models of the Zero-sen and the Hellcat never went into production. Mindful of the loss of performance with the gain in weight in later models of the A6M, and with decreased production of the Nakajima Sakae engine, the IJNAF's Koko Hombu finally, and belatedly, allowed Mitsubishi to install the more powerful Kinsei 62 engine in the Zero-sen. Now rated at 1,560hp for takeoff and 1,180hp at 19,000ft, the Kinsei 62 pushed the maximum speed

of the Zero-sen to 356mph, reversing the decline in its performance. The larger engine required the removal of the nose-mounted machine gun, so the new model, designated the A6M8 Model 63, mounted two 13.2mm Type 3 machine guns and two 20mm Type 99 cannon in the wings. The IJNAF took delivery of the first prototype of the A6M8 in May 1945, and after tests ordered 6,500 of the new fighters. The war ended before any were completed, however.

Grumman, too, mounted a more powerful engine on the last model of the Hellcat in the quest for greater performance. In mid-1944 it installed the more powerful C-Series Pratt & Whitney R-2800-18W radial in two F6Fs for tests as the XF6F-6. The C-Series generated 2,100hp for takeoff and 1,800hp at 23,000ft – 150hp more than the -10W engine in the F6F-5. With the new engine driving a four-bladed propeller, the XF6F-6 had a top speed of 407mph – the fastest of any Hellcat model. But by this time the XF8F-1 Bearcat – the intended replacement for the Hellcat – was about to enter its flight test program, which would reveal that the new fighter had a maximum speed of 424mph and rate of climb superior to the XF6F-6.

More importantly, the US Navy had found that with the R-2800-18W, the top speed of the F4U Corsair reached an even more impressive 446mph. With improvements to the Corsair finally making it acceptable as a carrier fighter, the US Navy decided to reserve R-2800-18W production for the Vought fighter as the F4U-4, so the XF6F-6 never went into production. Instead, fleet units continued to fly the F6F-5, with the F4U-4 being introduced into service with US Navy and US Marine Corps squadrons in early 1945.

Fastest of all Hellcats, the XF6F-6 with the Pratt & Whitney R-2800-18W engine had a maximum speed of 407mph, but the US Navy preferred the more capable F8F-1 Bearcat and decided to allocate the R-2800-18W engine to the Vought F4U-4 Corsair instead, as it had an even better performance than the XF6F-6. (Robert Lawson Collection, National Museum of Naval Aviation)

American and Japanese Fighter Production 1943–45					
	F6F	F4U	A6M	J2M	N1K1/2-J
1943	2,547	2,293	2,789	90	72
1944	6,140	5,380	3,830	274	891
1945	3,578	3,459	1,715	116	450
Total	12,265	11,132	8,334	480	1,413

(Source – United States Strategic Bombing Survey/Dean: *America's Hundred Thousand*)

FURTHER READING

Brown, Capt Eric "Winkle", *Wings of the Navy – Testing British and US Carrier Aircraft* (Hikoki Publications, 2013)

Gunston, Bill, *The Development of Piston Aero Engines* (Patrick Stephens Ltd, 1997)

Hata, Ikuhio, Yasuho Izawa and Christopher Shores, *Japanese Naval Air Force Fighter Units and their Aces 1932–1945* (Grub Street, 2011)

Horikoshi, Jiro, *Eagles of Mitsubishi – The Story of the Zero Fighter* (University of Washington, 1981)

Iwai, Tsutomu, *Kubo Reisen Tai – Sentoki Sojyu Jyu-nen no Kiroku* (Carrier Fighter Reisen – The Record of Piloting the Fighter Over Ten Years) (Kyonowadaisha, 1987)

Meyer, Corwin "Corky" and Steve Ginter, *Grumman F6F Hellcat,* Naval Fighters No 92 (Ginter Books, 2012)

Mikesh, Robert C., *Zero – Combat and Development History of Japan's Legendary Mitsubishi A6M Zero Fighter* (Motorbooks International, 1994)

Miller, Edward S., *War Plan Orange – The US Strategy to Defeat Japan, 1897-1945* (Naval Institute Press, 1991)

Minoru, Akimoto, *Reisen Ku Senki-Vol 2 – Reisen no Kobo* (Chronicle of the Reisen Battles-Vol 2 – Rise and Fall of the Reisen) (Kojinsha, 2010)

Minoru, Akimoto, *Reisen Ku Senki-Vol 3 – Fukutsu no Reisen* (Chronicle of the Reisen Battles-Vol 3 – The Unyielding Reisen) (Kojinsha, 2010)

Minoru, Akimoto, *Reisen Ku Senki-Vol 4 – Reisen no Shito* (Chronicle of the Reisen Battles-Vol 4 – The Reisen's Desperate Struggle), (Kojinsha, 2010)

Newton, Wesley Phillips and Robert R. Rea, Eds, *Wings of Gold – An Account of Naval Aviation Training in World War II: The Correspondence of Aviation Cadet/ Ensign Robert R. Rea* (University of Alabama Press, 1987)

Okumiya, Masatake and Jiro Horikoshi, with Martin Caidin, *The Zero Fighter* (Cassell, 1958)

Okumiya, Masatake and Jiro Horikoshi, with Martin Caidin, *Zero! The Story of the Japanese Navy Air Force 1937–1945* (Cassell, 1957)

Peattie, Mark R., *Sunburst – The Rise of Japanese Naval Air Power, 1909–1941* (Naval Institute Press, 2001)

Reynolds, Clark G., *The Fast Carriers – The Forging of an Air Navy* (McGraw-Hill, 1968)

Stafrace, Charles, *Warpaint Series No 84 – Grumman F6F Hellcat* (Warpaint Books, 2011)

Tillman, Barrett, *Hellcat – The F6F in World War II* (Naval Institute Press, 1979)

Tillman, Barrett, *US Navy Fighter Squadrons in World War II* (Specialty Press, 1997)

White, Graham, *R-2800 – Pratt & Whitney's Dependable Masterpiece* (Airlife, 2001)

Williams, Anthony G. and Dr Emmanuel Gustin, *Flying Guns of World War II – Development of Aircraft Guns, Ammunition, and Installations 1933–1945* (Airlife, 2003)

Willmott, H. P., *The War with Japan – The Period of Balance May 1942–October 1943* (SR Books, 2002)

Wooldridge, E. T., *Carrier Warfare in the Pacific – An Oral History Collection* (Smithsonian Press, 1993)

Yohoyama, Tamotsu, *Reisen Ichi-dai – Reisen Tai Kusen Shimatsu Ki* (Ah, The First Generation of the Reisen – The Record of the Reisen Fighter's Air Battles) (Kojinsha, 1992)

INDEX

References to illustrations are shown in **bold**.